Youth and Exploitation

Alan W. McEvoy
Wittenberg University

and

Edsel L. Erickson
Professor Emeritus, Western Michigan University

Lp Learning Publications, Inc.
MONTREAL   HOLMES BEACH, FL

Learning Publications, Inc.
P.O. Box 1338
Holmes Beach, Florida 34218-1338

Library of Congress Card Catalog Number 89-084978

Paperback: ISBN #1-55691-042-8

Year: 4 3 2 1 0   Print: 8 7 6 5 4 3 2 1

Printed in the United States of America

Contents

to

Carol, Cindy, Fritz, Ingrid,
Karl, Katy, Kyle and Ruth

On Being Used

Much has been written about people who selfishly use others without regard for the harm they inflict. Studies abound about the unfeeling character of those who economically, socially, physically and psychologically exploit their peers and family. What is not commonly understood is the nature of psychological exploitation or the character of the pain and damage experienced by victims, especially when the victimizers are close family members and peers. The price of this victimization is modestly expressed in such statements as: "You used my life to prove to yourself who you are" and "I was used".

Our discussion is about the character of exploitation in the intimate relationships of family and so-called friends. It is about the many overlooked ways in which exploitation is enacted and the damaging outcomes of that exploitation as victims attempt to cope with the selfishness of parents and friends.

It is true that most of us are selfish at one time or another. This is not our concern. Our attention is on exploitation when it is intense, consistent and seriously damaging to the psyches of its victims. We are concerned with exploitation that often is denied, yet repeated again and again.

Our focus is also limited to young people who, in a stage of emotional immaturity, are vulnerable. Much of this exploitation is so subtle that few parents or friends are aware of their power in producing seriously maladaptive behaviors in their children or friends.

We do not imply that all youth suicide, running away, drug abuse or violence is the result of parental or peer exploitation, but much is. There are, of course, multiple forces that impact on the health of young people. Nevertheless, we believe that exploitation is not a secondary problem. It is a primary cause behind the common condition of many young people in crisis.

The theme of this book—how exploitation is at the center of the personal despair among many of our young people—is not a totally new idea; but it is worthy of being reconsidered in light of the growing numbers of young people who are at the point of suicide, drug abuse, running away or violence.

1

The Perils
of Adolescence

- Approximately two out of three teenagers will experiment with illicit drugs.

- About one-third of all female adolescents are at some time sexually assaulted by a date.

- Over 7,000 young people in North America commit suicide each year.

Of all age groups, teenagers face the highest risk of being maimed, sexually assaulted, emotionally terrorized, or otherwise harmed because of someone's selfishness. Many are killed, and many more are physically and emotionally impaired by exploitive parents or peers. In addition, caring parents—persons who work hard at being good parents——often unintentionally push their children into the grasps of abusive and exploitive peers. Add to this the thousands of teenagers who contribute to their own harm by running away, abusing drugs or worse, attempting suicide and one can draw a shocking conclusion: the period of adolescence is a time of great danger.

> *   **Over half of all teenage deaths are associated with alcohol or drug usage.**

When one considers the kinds of trauma teenagers experience, the picture is sad. Every day in the United States and Canada, more than 9 teenagers are killed and more than 400 teenagers are seriously injured in alcohol-related automobile accidents. The National Council on Alcoholism reports that nearly 100,000 ten and eleven year old children get drunk at least once a week. As children enter their teens, the pressure to drink increases.

Teenagers who use illicit drugs are often subjected to poisons of which they are unaware. For example, the use of cocaine processed with a dry cleaning agent—an increasingly common practice—is resulting in brain damage. Likewise, highly potent and often lethal "designer drugs" are flooding the marketplace. These drugs are produced in "underground" labs without the benefit of tests for purity or for resulting harmful side effects.

> *   **According to current rates, approximately 25% of all teenage females will become teenage mothers.**

Among teenage mothers, the overwhelming majority will have out-of-wedlock births, and 96% will keep their babies.

Approximately 80% of these teenage mothers will drop out of high school. There is an extremely strong correlation between being a teenage parent, low educational attainment, and living in poverty. There is also an increased risk that these teenagers will become the victims of assault and battery. Furthermore, the infant children of these teenagers are likely to be caught in the cycle of violence by first becoming victims of abuse, and then when older, becoming abusers.

• **Over a quarter of a million students are attacked at school in a typical month.**

The "Safe School Study" conducted by the National Institute of Education which reported the above finding concluded that the victimization of teenagers is common in schools nearly everywhere. Threats, the use of obscenities, robbery and theft, physical assaults, and other forms of intimidation occur on a daily basis in both middle- and lower-class schools. Few teenagers are immune to being assaulted or robbed in school. The study claimed that over 2.4 million secondary school students are victims of theft each month, and that 800,000 students stay home from school at least one day per month out of fear.

• **Over one million teenagers run away from home annually.**

Runaway and homeless youth most often come from seriously disturbed home situations. Many are the victims of physical, sexual, or emotional abuse. Yet living on the streets imposes other serious risks such as drug abuse, prostitution, AIDS, delinquency, and physical assault. Current estimates suggest that there are between 300,000 and 500,000 "hard core" homeless teenagers living on the streets in the U.S. alone.

Existence for this group is so severe that as many as 20% attempt suicide.

- **At least 13% of all seventeen-year-olds are functionally illiterate.**

To be illiterate makes survival without crime that much more difficult in a society with a high standard of living. More than 25% of all teenagers do not graduate from high school. These semi-literate and unprepared young people are the least likely to find employment, either immediately or later as adults, and are most likely to become dependent on welfare. This group is over-represented in statistics on juvenile and adult crime, both as victims and as offenders.

These risks to teenagers described above are but a small portion of the increasing perils that are faced by all teenagers. Clearly, the troubles of adolescence are not confined to a specific social class or to a given racial, ethnic or religious group. Neither is the exploitation of teenagers restricted to rural or urban settings. Teenagers everywhere are at risk.

Of course, an awareness that teenagers are at risk is not new. Hundreds of books and articles have been written on acquaintance rape, teenage suicide, incest, physical battering at home, runaways, and substance abuse. However, little has been written on the one common experience that nearly all abused teenagers share: the experience of exploitation by parents, other adults or their peers.

Regardless of the specific details of their abuse, nearly all teenage victims have been used for other people's gratification. They have been exploited. In the following chapters, the subtle characteristics of exploitive relationships in the family and among peers are discussed at length. These relationships are examined in depth because few exploitive parents or friends recognize how they exploit, or realize the damage they are causing to others, to themselves, or to society.

There is another reason for this book. Many people do not recognize the critical differences in how teenagers are abused as contrasted to the abuse of younger children. In many respects, emotional, physical or sexual exploitation at home during the teenage period is much more like spouse abuse than the abuse of younger children. In both adolescent and spouse abuse, there tend to be premeditation and violent or severe attempts at domination. In contrast, the abuse of younger children tends to be spontaneous and reflective of inappropriate learning by parents regarding the raising of children.

Another difference between abused adolescents and young children is that fathers are more likely to be abusers of their teenage children than are mothers. The reverse is true with young children where mothers are somewhat more likely to be the abusers.

Slightly less than one-half of all abused teenagers have been exploited since early childhood. Typically, this group suffers unusually severe mental problems. Many are unable to trust adults or authority figures. They are unable to establish healthy relationships with anyone unless they receive considerable help from therapists. Furthermore, they are likely to become like their abusers in that they become extremely exploitive or violent toward others who are defenseless.

Yet, most teenagers who have experienced parental abuse were not abused before age thirteen. Usually, because their first serious abuse occurred later in life, the damage they incurred was not as great as that experienced by teenagers who had been abused since early childhood. Nonetheless, the damage that can be done to teenagers whose emotional, physical or sexual exploitation only begins in adolescence can be severe.

One other important difference is that abused children are highly sympathetic figures who evoke strong feelings of empathy from adults. Children are not seen as deserving of mistreatment. When it is known that children are severely abused, most caring adults want to intervene on their behalf. On the other hand, abused teenagers are viewed with suspicion and hostility by many adults. The tendency is to see adolescents as victimizers rather than as victims. They are seen as responsible for their own plight.

It is also true that some teenagers are violent and dangerous. The high rate of violent crime among juveniles is a sad fact which serves to increase the suspicions adults have of teenagers as a group. However, violent and exploitive teenagers are themselves often the products of violence and exploitation. Yet, whether they are victims or victimizers, most adults prefer to distance themselves from adolescents. Thus, when teenagers are in peril, the likelihood that adults will intervene on their behalf is low.

Even when teenagers are not victimized at home—and most are not—other adults or their peers are often dangerously abusive and exploitive. Abuse and exploitation from peers range from bullying, to date rape, to intense pressures to use drugs and alcohol, and to felonious criminal acts. And as children enter the teenage years, the attraction to their peers and the power of their peers to be exploitive dramatically increases. Unfortunately, most peer exploitation, like parental exploitation, is not recognized as such. Teenagers simply fail to see, in many cases, what others are doing to them.

What can be done about the exploitation of teenagers? First, one must understand the nature of the exploitation that most abused teenagers share. It is also important to understand the kinds of turmoil that result from being exploited. From such understandings, solutions can be offered for reducing the pain and suffering of millions of young people and their families.

Understanding the nature of exploitation also offers a way of diminishing major costs to society. These costs from the mistreatment of teenagers are reflected in higher taxes, more crime, lost production, and wasted human resources. All people pay a price when teenagers are exploited to satisfy the selfishness of others.

2

Exploitive Parents

Most parents love their children; they strive to protect their children from any harm which might befall them. Yet under their own roofs, many of these parents unintentionally engage in fundamentally destructive behaviors toward their offspring.

Rather than using persuasion to influence their children, some parents tend to rely on the use of intimidation or violence to get their way. The worst of the parents tend to be untrustworthy, undependable, and abusive. Perhaps most damaging of all, abusive parents tend to be exploitive, or what some refer to as "users." They use their children for their own ends, often without due regard for the injuries they cause. In other words, they exploit the very people to whom they are most attached. Perhaps this is why the "user phenomenon" among parents is the most misunderstood feature of abuse.

USER RELATIONSHIPS

To be a "user" is to exploit others for selfish and harmful ends. A father who molests his daughter is misusing his power and position of trust. He is making her serve his felt interests without proper regard for her needs. In simple terms, he is being selfish and exploitive. He is causing her injury. The relationship between the incestuous father and his daughter is characterized by an imbalance of power. The father's interest is in what the daughter can do for him, without consideration of the costs to her. Thus, his daughter is his victim. She is treated by him as merely an object for serving his gratification. This is an obvious example of exploitation.

Other cases of exploitation are not as obvious, yet are common. Consider, for example, the mother who subtly threatens to withhold her love unless her child does something that is only for the mother's benefit. The fear of rejection by one's parents is a strong force among children, even when they are teenagers. In fact, one of the typical ways that teenagers are intimidated is by a threatened loss of parental affection. When parental love is dispensed conditionally, it creates in children insecurity rather than security, guilt and distrust rather than confidence and acceptance. In this sense, parental love is used as a technique of manipulation rather than being an end in itself.

An indirect act of parental intimidation is when parents use their child's friends or other family members to exploit their child. An extreme example of this is a father who tells his adolescent daughter that if she doesn't engage in sex with him, he will have sex with her sister; or if she tells on him, the family will break up and her mother will no longer love her. The daughter is coerced to do what her father wants out of her concern for other people in her life.

What is the most typical injury with which abusers threaten their victims? The answer is not threatened or actual physical harm. Rather, the most common and powerful force that exploitive parents use is to threaten their children with a loss of their love. Fear of rejection is a very potent force in the exploitation of adolescents. When threats of rejection are coupled with other forms of exploitation, such as physical or sexual abuse, the consequences for the victim are both long term and devastating.

A seeming contradiction exists in the relationships between exploitive parents and their children. Threats of being rejected are usually coupled with rewards. These rewards can be either unintended on the part of the offending parents, or they may be meant to be compensation for temporary feelings of remorse, or they may be intended to promote the continuation of exploitation. In the case of incest, victims may be given gifts or other special favors. However, these rewards, no matter how special, do not adequately compensate teenagers for the harm done to them.

Exploitive relationships of parents with their offspring are different from healthy parent-child relationships where there is mutual benefit. The main benefits for healthy parents are love and the satisfaction of knowing that they have tried to help their children. For children of emotionally healthy parents, the benefits, among others, are feelings of security, trust, and the ability to share their feelings with others. These teenagers, like their healthy parents, know how to love and to be loved by others.

On the other hand, at the heart of a user relationship is a fundamental selfishness. Extremely abusive and exploitive parents are so concerned with satisfying their own desires that they cannot or will not consider the interests, feelings, or needs of their children.   In such cases, the preferences of exploitive parents dominate.   During the period that the abuse takes place, there is a serious absence of sympathy.   Only after the abuse period is over does remorse sometimes occur. Remorse, however, is seldom sufficient to prevent the next attack from coming; neither is feeling sorry sufficient to undo the damage.   This is because abusive parents have tendencies that prevent them from recognizing in themselves their exploitive character.

TENDENCIES OF ABUSIVE PARENTS

While there are unique features among abusive parents, nearly all share certain characteristics.   Abusive parents tend to:

- **deny** any responsibility for their actions;

- **blame** their victims, saying it was "his or her fault";

- exhibit **hypocrisy** in that they "preach" one thing and do another;

- have a high need to **dominate** their children;

- hold a deep **mistrust** of their children;

- show an obsessive concern for their **own felt needs** and almost no concern for the needs and rights of their children; and

- **repeat** abusive acts compulsively.

Denial

Among the most common characteristics of abusive people, is their failure to recognize or to admit that their behavior is abusive. It is like "wearing blinders," particularly at the time they are abusive. No parent wants to admit responsibility for harming his or her child. Even in the face of considerable evidence that their actions are injurious, most abusive parents will deny their abuse, or minimize the negative consequences of their actions. There are several reasons for this denial.

One reason, as mentioned, is that exploitive parents often care dearly about their children, even though they exploit them. To be sure, one can be exploitive or abusive of a loved one. Loving one's child makes it extremely painful to admit that one has been abusive. To avoid such an admission is a way of avoiding feelings of guilt and depression. Even when parents are directly responsible for their children committing suicide, running away, or abusing drugs, they will deny their role as a way of reducing their pain. They will be at a loss to explain why their child killed him or herself. To facilitate this denial in the case of suicide, for example, physicians often list conditions other than suicide as the cause of death. Many teenage suicides are officially labeled as accidents.

Another reason for parental denial is that by admitting responsibility for being abusive, a psychological pressure is created to behave differently toward their children. This means that abusive parents who admit to being abusive must change habits upon which they have come to rely. Much like any other addiction, exploitive and abusive parents become so attached to certain habits of disciplining their children that it is hard for them to believe that change is possible or desirable. Denying the harm of their conduct relieves them from the prospect of having to alter how they act.

It is interesting to note that many abusive parents convince themselves that the real harm comes not from continuing a set of injurious actions toward their children, but rather from changing their behaviors. For example, a parent who comes to be dependent upon using verbal chastisement or physical violence to "motivate" a child, usually believes that no other method of discipline will work. To use less extreme or different forms of control is viewed by these parents as counterproductive. For such parents, emotional or physical violence is rationalized as beneficial to their children rather than as injurious. In other words, rationalization for abusive behavior takes the form of believing that one is doing it for the good of the victim. Popular cliches such as "I'm doing it for your own good," or "This will make a man out of you," illustrate such rationalizations. These rationalizations are a way of denying harm and of feeling justified for having been abusive.

It should be pointed out that even when parents admit to having inflicted harm, they can still engage in denial. They may not deny the harm they caused, but rather they deny their intentions to harm. For example, getting drunk is often a necessary preliminary for an incestuous father to sexually abuse his child. Even though he realizes the harm done, the drunkenness becomes a convenient excuse to "save face" and to deny that he is "that kind of person." Such denials allow parents to use their children in an exploitive way, and yet be convinced that it happened because of circumstances "beyond their control." Their denial thus frees them from having to confront their self-centeredness.

Consider how often abusers will try to explain their actions with a phrase such as "I'm not really like that . . . I only did it because I was drunk." By employing such excuses, the abuser is able to avoid coming to terms with the deeper truths of his or her exploitive actions. Thus, denial is a common strategy for avoiding responsibility, for saving face, and for failing to see the negative consequences of one's exploitations of others. Denial thereby provides a psychological basis for continued exploitation.

Persuasive denial by abusive parents is a means for not only being absolved from feelings of responsibility, it is also a means for manipulating the perceptions of others outside of the family. If the denials are believed, the parent is cast in a more favorable light. The end result of these denials is to allow exploitive parents to continue their exploitation for months or years without others intervening. And if their child runs away or commits suicide, the exploitive parents and others may even wonder why, failing to acknowledge their responsibility.

Blaming Their Victim

It is seemingly easy, if not logical, for exploitive parents to point the finger of blame at their children. For example, a typical stepfather who sexually molests his ten-year-old step-daughter will claim that she was being "seductive" or had subtly invited his "special sexual attention." Another example is the violent parent who states that "It's your fault for making me so angry." Another very common example is an alcoholic parent who blames the child for causing him or her to drink. By blaming the child, the offending parent shifts the attention of both the child and others away from his or her abusive behavior. Blaming the victim is also a way by which exploitive parents deny responsibility for their actions. Taken together, denial and blame are the fuel of exploitive relationships.

Hypocrisy

Another pattern among exploitive parents is to engage in hypocritical behaviors relevant to the abuse. "Do as I say, not as I do." An alcoholic parent who dwells on the dangers of drinking, or a sexually abusive parent who often "preaches" about the immorality of intimate relationships, fits into this category. It is typical for exploitive parents to serve as hypocritical role models. Their actions are in direct opposition to the ideal values they claim, as well as to those of society. Sadly, few users ever see the contradictions in their behavior. Ironically, many users view themselves as paragons of morality, pointing the finger elsewhere for the very harm that they cause.

Domination

It is also common for severely exploitive parents to demand unyielding submission to their authority and to their needs. They tend to be domineering people. An abuser's "authority" allows for no challenge. The mentality of exploitive parents is one where their children are expected, indeed demanded, to do exactly as told, even down to the minutest detail. Even the most unreasonable requests take on the aura of a commandment. Indeed, when a teenager fails to submit to such parental domination, the abusive parent often responds with extreme anger and overly severe punishment. Failure to submit to parental domination, however unreasonable, is then used by the parent to feel justified in blaming the victim for the abuse.

Mistrust

Another characteristic of exploitive parents is a basic mistrust of their teenage children. This mistrust is particularly evident when their teenagers are outside of their immediate control (e.g., on dates, at school or with friends). Such mistrust is a direct result of the exploitive parents' desire to maintain a shroud of secrecy concerning their abuse. Any event or interaction which might reveal the abuse to "outsiders" is suspect.

Not only is the teenager mistrusted by his or her exploitive parents, but so too are the teenage victim's friends or relatives who are in a position to learn the truth. As a result, the offending parent often attempts to isolate his or her teenager from others, especially if there is a perceived risk of discovery. This is similar to spouse abuse. By attempting to isolate his or her teenage child, the abusive parent seeks to avoid detection and to be able to perpetuate the abuse. An abuser simply cannot afford to trust others to know about his or her child's predicament.

Violations of Rights

In conjunction with exhibiting distrust, exploitive parents regularly intrude in a highly exaggerated manner on the freedoms of their teenage children and their children's peers. Frequent interrogations of peers and other family members concerning the actions of their teenage children, invasions of privacy, and a denial of basic human rights are common aspects of offending parents. Again, these intrusions are designed to maintain control over their children and to keep any abuse secret. A typical example of such intrusive surveillance is the sexually abusive father who monitors virtually all of his daughter's activities, and jealously interrogates dating partners and friends about her outside associations. Other examples include opening their children's mail and spying on them. Violations of rights are thus one of the chief mechanisms by which exploitive parents keep their offspring isolated from those who might otherwise be in a position to intervene.

Compulsive Repetition of Abusive Acts

One of the most harmful dimensions of an exploitive parent's relationship with his or her child is when abusive behavior is compulsively repeated. Whatever kind of abuse the exploitive parent engages in, it often takes on a ritualistic aspect. By "ritualistic" it is meant that there is a sequence of events before, during and after the abusive episode which are repeated over and over again. While the sequence will vary from user to user, each abuser tends to follow a pattern. For example, an incestuous father might repeatedly start a sequence by first getting drunk, then finding an excuse for getting his daughter alone, molesting her in the same way as before, going to sleep, awakening and giving her gifts, and finally, acting as if nothing ever happened.

Furthermore, once a pattern is established, the frequency and the intensity of the abuse tends to escalate. Without deliberate outside intervention or the incapacitation of the offender, there is little likelihood that the abuse will abate. Only rarely is victimization ended by the victim being able to mobilize sufficient resources to finally make an escape. The longer the abuse continues, the greater the likelihood for the victims to experience long-term trauma. Also, the longer the abuse continues, the more difficult it is for victims to extricate themselves.

One final observation regarding exploitive relationships can be made. It is probably true that most relationships between parents and their children, including healthy relationships, will at times involve some selfishness.   Yet there are several key considerations which distinguish abusive parents from relatively healthy parents.   With exploitive parents, the abuse occurs frequently, is severe in intensity, and it continues for long periods of time, even years.   Moreover, the harm done to teenagers is often conscious and intentional, despite denials to the contrary.   Even in light of having caused obvious injury (e.g., a severely battered teenager), these parents tend not to change how they behave toward their children.   To better illustrate these patterns, it is useful to examine a common, yet not well understood, form of teenage exploitation . . . incest.

3

Incest:
A Special Case
of Exploitation

Sexual abuse, and incest in particular, engenders such intense feelings of moral outrage that impartiality is difficult. Although there is considerable variation in what people think about various sexual practices, our society has established stringent taboos against incest. Depending upon who is rendering judgment, incest ranges from carnal discussions of sex with children, to acts of exhibitionism, molestation and rape. As shown in the following chart, there is also a range of damage that occurs from incest depending on the degree of threat and force used.

INCEST

LEAST DAMAGING
(Assault; threat
alone)

TYPES OF INCEST *

- Non-coital sexual contact
  (e.g., French kissing,
  petting, fondling)

- Exhibitionism (exposure of
  offender's sexual organs)

- Voyeurism (watching victims
  undress, nude)

- Masturbatory contact with
  genitals

- Fellatio, cunnilingus

- Penetration with penis or objects

Involves different
treatment plans,
prognoses, ages, time
sequences, consequences
(legal and
psychological), and
dynamics (homosexual,
heterosexual, close
relative, distant
relative, related by
marriage).

MOST DAMAGING
Battery & Assault:
i.e., physical force
combined with threat

*   Adapted by permission of the publisher from INCEST by
    Adele Mayer: Learning Publications, Inc., Holmes Beach,
    Florida, 1985.

While such characterizations of incest as described in the chart may sensitize one to the problem, there is still dispute as to when incest occurs. Given the lack of agreement in stating when incest occurs, it is little wonder that statistics concerning its incidence vary.

In the United States, estimates of sexually abusive behavior between adults and children vary between 200,000 and 10 million cases per year. While it is impossible to determine the exact incidence of incest, evidence consistently shows that sexual abuse cases involve parents and surrogate parents more than strangers. In only about 3 to 10 percent of sexual abuse cases are the sexually abusive perpetrators strangers to their victims.

PATTERNS OF INCEST

Incest differs from physical abuse in two important respects. First, incest tends to be premeditated while physical abuse alone by parents tends to be more spontaneous. Secondly, incest is a serious taboo. Whereas a large portion of society supports the practice of hitting children in the name of discipline, most people do not condone incest. However, both the hitting of children and incest are alike in that they tend to occur over an extended period of time (months or years).

Stepfathers and surrogate fathers, followed by fathers, are by far the most common sexual abusers of children, accounting for over 80 percent of the reported cases. Mother-son or mother-daughter sexual relationships are relatively rare. Given the high proportion of stepfather and surrogate father involvement, the number of children living under this arrangement is significant and increasing. About 50% of all eighteen-year-olds have lived parts of their lives in a family with a stepfather or surrogate father.

The onset of incest can begin at any age and can happen to males as well as to females. However, the "typical" victim of incest is female and is first subjected to incestuous behavior between the ages of 8 and 12. From the first experience, she is made to continue in a pattern of victimization which lasts over a prolonged period of time. Younger incest victims are likely to experience fondling, oral-genital stimulation, and exhibitionism rather than penetration. Then teenagers, unlike younger children, are likely to experience penetration. Physical violence is seldom used to force teens into incest. Threats of rejection or loss of love, and making the victim feel guilty and responsible, are the most common means of fathers or surrogate fathers forcing incest.

There are at least two basic reasons for a general absence of physical force in incest. In the first case, incestuous fathers need to enlist the cooperation of their children to keep them available as sexual "partners" for an extended period of time, and not leave any physical evidence which might lead to discovery. To physically damage one's child in an observable way would diminish the chances of such cooperation and increase the likelihood of discovery.

Second, teenagers are still susceptible to a parent's position of psychological, physical, and material dominance. Incestuous parents use loyalty, trust, and dependence as weapons to force their children into sexual activity and to ensure their silence. With such an arsenal of psychological weapons to manipulate the victim, physical force seldom is required.

The fear of possible family disintegration often serves as motivation for a teenager's cooperation with an incestuous parent. Such fear is a frequently cited reason why victims of incest fail to divulge their having been sexually abused, but is not the initial reason for becoming involved. This is not to suggest in any way that teenage victims of incest give their consent, or are responsible for sexual involvement with their parents. Indeed, there is no solid research evidence to suggest that teenagers instigate incestuous liaisons with their parents.

As in the case of rape, there are stereotypes and false assumptions concerning the degree of victim-precipitation of the experience. Some have incorrectly asserted that incest victims are being "seductive" or are spontaneously acting out sexual fantasies. Similarly offered is the false observation that children enjoy the "special attention" of incest and therefore bear partial responsibility. Some false claims are made purporting that daughters welcome the sexual advances of their fathers as an indication of parental love.

Meaningful consent to engage in sexual practices with their parents is not a legal or morally logical possibility, either among young children or teenagers. Children are not responsible for incest, adult offenders are. It is the adults who misuse their power, and it is their children who pay the price of that abuse. Adult abusers use their position of power to instigate incest, to continue the practice once it has started, to keep their behavior secret, and ultimately to blame their victims for what happened.

Yet another popular, though untested, belief places considerable responsibility on the mother for father-daughter incest. This theory purports that it is the mother's "unconscious desire" to place the daughter in the role of wife and lover, thus relieving herself of this responsibility. According to this false argument, by abandoning her responsibilities as a wife and mother, the mother pushes the father and daughter into a sexual relationship.

In truth, however, research supports the view that the overwhelming majority of mothers do not consciously or unconsciously encourage their husbands to enter into incestuous relationships with their daughters. The untested theory that mothers initiate involvement carries a sexist overtone. The sexist overtone is that of blaming women for the inappropriate conduct of men. Such a sexist attitude functions to make it difficult to help victims and their families. This argument also fails to explain male victims of incest.

Restated, while it is true that incest is indicative of a breakdown of the family, neither children nor mothers cause this breakdown. It is true that in some cases mothers come to know about incestuous relationships, and, for a variety of reasons, they reject or fail to act upon this knowledge. Even when they fail to act against the incestuous father, however, to blame the woman or teenager and not the father for the incest is wrong.

FACTORS CONTRIBUTING TO INCEST

Although simple theories concerning the causes of incest abound, the problem is complex. No single explanation is sufficient to account for all cases. In truth, there is considerable variation between and among users, victims, and family interaction patterns. Nonetheless, there are certain conditions that are relatively common to incest situations. These include psychological isolation, stress and alcohol abuse.

Psychological Isolation

Similar to the general pattern of physical abuse cases, isolation is frequently cited as a cause of incest. Isolation does not necessarily mean physical separation, but rather is determined by the lack of close friendships outside the family. In nearly all cases, an overly heavy dependence upon one another within the family appears to be crucial. Often there is deep suspicion of "outsiders." Also, once a pattern of incest begins, a feared stigma of public disclosure tends to further isolate the family. This isolation further intensifies the incestuous pattern and reduces the likelihood of outside intervention.

Some argue that a lack of "legitimate" sexual outlets can result in the development of incest within the family. Evidence indicates that this is wrong. Most offending fathers have "legitimate" sexual outlets, but nonetheless choose to misuse their children sexually. Sexual dysfunction in a marriage is not the cause of incest——selfishness is. The presence of incest, however, can produce sexual difficulties in a marriage. It can greatly complicate the development of healthy sexual patterns among victims.

Given the lack of an external support system, there is heavy dependence on family members to meet emotional and sexual needs. It should also be noted that with genetically related incest perpetrators, it is not a generalized pedophilic craving for children that initially leads to incest, though such a craving may subsequently develop. However, in the case of stepparents, pedophilia is a somewhat more common causal factor. And it is true that a pedophiliac sometimes marries or lives with a woman for the purpose of gaining access to her children.

It should be pointed out that isolation is not a true "cause" of incest. Rather, isolation constitutes a background condition which makes the emergence of incest possible. Isolation provides an opportunity for users to act in secrecy, and to seek emotional and sexual gratification from those most available and vulnerable–their children.

Alcohol

Another commonly attributed factor in incest is alcohol abuse. As many as 50% of reported cases of incest involve an alcoholic father. However, as in the case of physical abuse, it is unlikely that alcohol "causes" the incestuous behavior. Rather, alcohol lowers inhibitions and provides a convenient excuse or face-saving rationalization for the conduct. Users employ this as an excuse to deny their conduct. Like other personal maladjustment problems, alcoholism may be as much a result as it is a cause of incest. Furthermore, most alcoholic fathers do not molest their children.

Climates of Stress

The occurrence of incest is both symptomatic of, and a catalyst for family stress. Marital discord and sexual incompatibility between husband and wife, economic difficulty, illness, prolonged absence followed by the return of the father, fear of abandonment, family disintegration, and the death of a spouse, have all been cited as reasons for incest. However, stress alone does not cause incest. There are too many people who experience extreme stress, without incest, to accept such an explanation. Nonetheless, the presence of incest is a source of extreme stress within a family.

We know that most incestuous parents experience considerable personal problems. The observation of such tensions and personal problems may be the basis of a popular view that mental illness is the reason for incest. However, contrary to popular belief, there is little evidence to suggest that mental illness is the cause. Nevertheless, the fear, shame, guilt and low self-esteem associated with incest add considerable psychological stress to victims, to offenders, and to other family members. In other words, mental illness is as likely to be a result of incest as it is its cause.

EFFECTS OF SEXUAL ABUSE

Controversy exists over whether or not teenagers are seriously harmed by having their parents exploit them sexually, physically or emotionally. A few argue that the "innocence of youth" protects them against harm; that since youth are vague about what society expects, they are not traumatized by violations. For example, as Kinsey has stated: "It is difficult to understand why a child, except for its cultural conditioning, should be disturbed at having its genitals touched, or disturbed at seeing the genitals of other persons." However, there is overwhelming evidence that children and adolescents are harmed when they are sexually, physically or emotionally exploited.

Experts today point out that most people have been taught to feel that incest is wrong and sick. That is why adolescents and adults who experience incest are so secretive. Of course, most therapists recognize that being secretive about participating in an event which is a major societal taboo can cause deep psychological problems.

In fact, most mental health workers and researchers report that incest victims suffer so much from their denial that they are impaired long into adulthood. Furthermore, the psychological consequences of incest are much worse than those due to rape by strangers. The extensive confusion, fear, shame, low self-esteem, and thoughts of suicide among teenage incest victims are evidence of severe damages caused by incest. Indeed, studies indicate that a high percentage of women who undergo psychiatric treatment were sexually exploited during their childhood or adolescence. Accordingly, the Department of Health and Human Services in the United States issued a report that stated:

> "The fact that many women reveal their incestuous history while involved in therapy for other problems, suggests that the damage from child sexual abuse may be related to other problems from which they are seeking help. Depression and confusion about their own identities are common reactions of many victims. Some jump into early marriages as a means of escaping their family situations and dealing with their feelings of aloneness. Some report feeling 'marked' or stigmatized for life ..."

Unlike the effects of physical abuse and neglect, there are few obvious signs associated with a sexually maltreated teenager. Furthermore, incest victims are usually protective of their families and are not likely to be forthcoming about their experiences. When incestuous experiences are revealed, the revelations usually occur during a time when there is confrontation and crisis in the family. For instance, an adolescent may divulge incest if she has a fight with her father over her desires to date, or if her father initiates her younger sisters into incest.

Adolescent males who are sexually abused are especially prone to be secretive about their exploitation. Males in our society are expected to be able to "protect" themselves. To "allow" oneself to be violated is seen by the young male as a personal failure and as an indication of "weakness." Certainly, one does not make such a failure public.

Further compounding the problem is the fact that nearly always the perpetrator is an adult male. This adds great confusion to the male youngster's sense of sexual identity. Thus, adolescent males who are sexually exploited feel a double loss: they have lost their "manly" ability to defend themselves and they have lost their "manhood" in terms of their emerging sexuality. The stigma is such that many would rather endure a private hell than suffer the public humilation of what they perceive as their failure.

However, if a young male or female does reveal sexual assault, there is a tendency among adults to disregard the account. Unfortunately, Freud argued that children are prone to incestuous fantasies. As a result of this assertion about childhood fantasies, a teenager's revelation of sexual involvement with a parent is likely to be considered as a fabrication or an expression of fantasy. On the other hand, the data shows that a very small percentage of teenage initiated reports of sexual abuse are false. The problem is compounded by the fact that victims often retract their account upon further questioning. Such retractions occur because teenagers are terrified by the possible breakup of their families, by the embarrassment they will face with their friends, and by the feared severity of the punishment that they, their parents or friends will receive. In addition, in the interim between a report of incest and its investigation, the abusive parent has ample time to construct a "cover story" and to pressure the teenager into denial.

Regardless of whether or not a teenager reveals incest or other sexual assault, several cues exist for astute observers to use in discovering sexual maltreatment. To some extent, the physical and behavioral symptoms vary with the age of the victim. While no single characteristic is sufficient evidence of incest, a pattern of symptoms should raise the spectre of its existence.

The following are characteristics commonly seen among sexually abused teenage males or females:

1. behavioral problems such as running away, truancy, substance abuse, being withdrawn, and fits of crying;

2. inability to establish positive relationships with peers;

3. talk of being "dirty" or "damaged," excessive bathing, and very low self-esteem;

4. sexual promiscuity and prostitution;

5. frequent bacterial infection, genital rash, venereal disease or chronic vaginal discharge; and

6. phobias, fear of adults, hysterical seizures, psychosomatic illness, severe depression, and suicide attempts.

Teachers, school nurses, counselors and others should pay special attention to youth who are in high-risk groups. Those who are handicapped or retarded represent one such high risk category. Their peers often take advantage of them as do some parents. Also, in families where there is a previous history of sexual abuse by others, the younger children may become targets. Similarly, where there is frequent shifting of stepparents or live-in surrogates, the risk of sexual abuse seems to be greater. Where the mother is absent and the surrogate father or father is in close and secluded proximity to the daughter for long periods of time, the risk of sexual abuse greatly increases.

In the case of an adolescent female, an incestuous relationship may come to light if she becomes pregnant.

Although statistics vary, approximately seven to ten percent of female adolescent incest victims become pregnant.   Not only does this increase the risk of genetic problems if the pregnancy is carried to term, but the psychological risks to the victim are heightened by such a pregnancy regardless of whether the baby is born or not. Variables such as age, frequency of occurrence, and degree of physical force, are key factors in the amount of harm done to victims.

Many juveniles who run away from home, many youths involved in delinquency, large numbers of prostitutes, and many others who have emotional problems and have experienced sexual abuse need the special attention and care of therapists if their problems are to be reduced.   It is of paramount importance, therefore, that everyone understand the damages that can be done by parents to satisfy their sexual desires, and the need to get special professional help for victims of sexual abuse in the family.   Their problems are unique.   Moreover, incest victims share many of the same problems that teenage victims of other forms of parental abuse experience.

4

How Victims Feel

All teenage victims of parental exploitation, whether it is sexual, physical or emotional, have strong feelings of attachment to their parents, regardless of how they were victimized. Most victims love their parents. Ironically, however, teenage victims who love their parents can also be extremely attached to them by hatred. They can simultaneously love their parents and want to receive love from them, while at the same time hating and resenting their parents for what they are doing. These attachments, whether expressed in terms of love or hatred, reflect the fact that an exploitive parent demands extensive attention and creates a dependency situation that cannot be ignored. Even long into adulthood, after teenage victims have left home or their parents have died, attachments to their exploitive parents endure and continue to be major influences on their lives.

It is this love and hate, combined with exploitation, that have profound repercussions on the beliefs and behaviors of teenage victims. As a consequence of being exploited by those who are expected to act as loving protectors, it is common for victims to learn certain things about themselves and others. What do they learn? How do they perceive the world about them? How do they cope with the tremendous confusion they experience as a result of being exploited by their parents? Simply stated, victims of parental exploitation tend to respond with public denial, private rejection, insecurity, distrust, powerlessness, moral confusion, limited communication skills, feelings of psychological isolation, the "Stockholm Syndrome" and the "Oh woe is me" syndrome.

DENIAL

Children initially learn to accept their exploitive parents' view of events and publicly deny that their parents have done anything wrong. This helps to explain why exploited teenagers will protect their exploiters. The denials of abusive parents, reinforced by their children's denials, diminish the chances of the exploitation being discovered.

Teenage victims who try to cover up the wrongs done to them by their parents also tend to believe that their parents have a right to deny what they have done. It is typical for teenage victims to make comments such as "he only beats me when I need it" or "I'm really to blame for what she did to me."   An irony is that exploited teenagers feel guilty and suffer from depression for what others do to them, even though they are themselves blameless. Exploited teenagers who truly deny they are being exploited are merely trying to cope with a fundamental contradiction: their protectors are harming them.

There is a sad irony in such denial. Unconsciously, by denying their own victimization, these teenagers greatly increase the likelihood that they will be further exploited by their parents. They present themselves over and over to their abusing parents as targets because they do not have the physical, psychological or intellectual capability to resist. They are not in a position to grasp what is happening to them. They often lack the resources to escape or to seek the assistance of those who could intervene.

FEELINGS OF VIOLATION

While young abused children may deny, even to themselves, that their parents are abusive, abused teenagers gradually become wiser. They learn from their peers, teachers, films, and other sources that they have been abused. They experience the same tensions as anyone who has been violated, whether by a thief, a robber, a mugger, a rapist or any other violator of one's identity or belongings. They feel degraded and without dignity. These especially intense feelings of being degraded are heightened by having to deny their violation publicly. The denial means that one must "live a lie," thus contributing even further to one's sense of injustice. Perhaps this is why most therapists believe that the very first step in helping victims is to get them to admit that they have been exploited through no fault of their own.

FEELINGS OF INSECURITY

Another tragic outcome for teenagers who are exploited by their parents is the destruction of feelings of safety. Being harmed by parents removes from teenagers a sense of safety and replaces it with pervasive and lingering anxieties. These anxiety feelings are particularly pronounced if parental exploitation occurs over a long period of time.

Fears and anxieties may become so deeply embedded that the capacities of teenagers to perform even simple tasks are undermined. For example, teenage victims of parental abuse may be so inattentive and preoccupied that their school work suffers. Fears may also manifest themselves in eating disorders, nightmares, or various other behavioral problems. The point is that when teenagers feel unsafe, their normal functioning is hindered. Feeling safe is a basic prerequisite for competent functioning in virtually any situation. And when children and teenagers learn that their home is not a safe haven, it is difficult for them to believe that they can be safe anywhere.

FEELINGS OF DISTRUST

Another outcome for teenagers who are exploited by their parents is a profound loss of trust in their parents and in other people. Teenagers who are harmed by their parents often come to believe that no one is worthy of their trust. Their mistrust applies to strangers, to acquaintances, and even to persons who are deserving of their trust (such as those who would be good friends, teachers or counselors). For many teenage victims, being harmed by a parent constitutes a "core experience" wherein fear, distrust and emotional withdrawal are a means for survival. Once these responses of distrust develop, any relationship which might hold the potential of becoming emotionally intimate triggers a response of rejection. Unfortunately, such mistrust and rejection of others is usually long term and seldom changed without therapy.

Although it is an understandable reaction, any general deep-seated distrust of people makes it difficult to establish healthy relationships with others. Pervasive feelings of mistrust result in a diminished capacity to develop close and nurturing relationships. Bonds of caring, sympathy, empathy, mutual rapport, and mutual nurturance are all built upon foundations of trust. Unfortunately, most victims of exploitive parents suffer for years in silence, isolated from meaningful and loving relationships, because they have mistakenly learned that trusting others makes them vulnerable to even more exploitation.

FEELINGS OF POWERLESSNESS

Among the qualities that make a person effective in human relationships are feelings of security, mutual trust and sharing, as well as beliefs in the ability to influence what will happen in life. Being effective in living is based on a feeling that one has some control over his or her life. Feeling a sense of control over one's life is undermined when one endures exploitive parents. Victims feel that their fate is dictated by others. For them, there is a feeling that they can neither prevent nor escape the next episode of parental abuse. They feel powerless.

However, there will be some attempts by teenage victims of parental exploitation to control events. For many, as they strive to gain control, the only alternatives they see are to viciously fight back, to escape through drugs, to run away, or to commit suicide. Victims frequently will "act out," but they typically do so in ways which add to their problems.

If they fail to fight back or escape, what then? The result is indecisiveness, even lower self-esteem and cynical fatalism. For these victims, it may take years of effort to overcome a truncated sense of confidence in their ability to make decisions.

Such feelings of powerlessness usually impair their abilities to perform competently in every human relationship. Oftentimes, this lack of confidence in self is at the root of unhealthy dependency relationships with more assertive peers or other adults who, in turn, exploit them further. Who can say how many cases of teenage pregnancy, dating violence or substance abuse are related to unhealthy dependencies on their parents? What is certain is this: to weaken feelings of personal control and self-esteem among teenagers dramatically increases the risk of their entering into relationships outside the home which can be equally exploitive.

Also, adolescents who are emotionally, physically or sexually exploited by their parents are likely to encounter excessive attempts at parental domination. As a consequence, teenage victims are again made to feel powerless and unable to cope with their parents except by finding a way of hurting their parents or escaping. Such a sense of futility reduces the ability of teenage victims to interact with all authority figures, regardless of their legitimacy. The result is, again, one of two inappropriate extremes: almost total rejection or total submission to authority figures.

MORAL CONFUSION

It is an obvious truism: parents are, to their offspring, important role models. Their children tend to copy them. What happens when the behavior of parents is exploitive and is violent? What happens when parents abuse their teenage children and seemingly get away with it? A powerful message is conveyed to the children that it is all right to hurt others.

By getting away with hurting people, exploitive behavior by parents is made to seem acceptable, even when it is not. Abusive behaviors are legitimized by the exploitive parent, who makes exploitation appear as a normal—indeed a preferred— strategy for achieving what one desires. Little wonder that many exploited teenagers learn to become emotionally and physically abusive of others who are weaker. They learn to justify imposing their will on others. They learn to employ the same strategies of exploitation that others have used on them. They learn that power and intimidation, not kindness and consideration, are to be valued.

LIMITED COMMUNICATION SKILLS

Another common consequence of being exploited by one's parents is an impairment of communication skills. Seriously exploited teenagers often lack the ability to talk freely with adults and peers who can help them. While they suffer deep anxieties, they are unable to express how they feel. Thus, there is little likelihood of their asking for help, even when they are in serious need and help is available. Even amidst a crisis, the teenager often puts up such a "front" that adults are shocked when they finally learn the truth.

Exploited teenagers often anticipate that even if they do ask for help, they will not be believed. To make matters worse, if exploited adolescents wait a long period of time before reporting what has happened, their credibility is lowered. Adult authorities are not likely to believe teenagers who wait to report on their abusive parents. When one delays in revealing abuse, it often results in others interpreting these belated accounts as lies or as attempts to hide complicity.

Hence, abused teenagers come to feel that not only do others not understand, but they believe that they can't communicate to others what they feel.

FEELINGS OF ISOLATION

It is important to understand that an exploited person's lack of communication skills, in concert with denial, moral confusion, lost safety, lost trust and limited autonomy, usually results in feelings of being "alone in the world." Feeling "alone" of course, does not mean that one is physically separate from others or that one can not establish any relationships with peers or other adults.

Indeed, feeling alone or like an outsider at home can literally drive one to seek some form of gratification with peers. Yet there is no guarantee that peers or others will not be equally exploitive. In fact, many teenagers will enter into disastrous dating relationships or become involved with delinquent gangs while trying to escape their parents.

Isolation from one's parents is also related to isolation from other family members. It is relatively common for siblings who are not the direct victims of abuse to isolate their abused brothers or sisters psychologically. Oftentimes, children learn from their exploitive mothers or fathers to blame their brothers or sisters for causing family turmoil. They learn to engage in "scapegoating." Thus, siblings can help to cause their brothers or sisters to be "loners" in the family.

These so called "non-abused" siblings may also learn to keep the situation of their abused sister or brother a secret. Ironically, by maintaining the secret of their brother's or sister's abuse, these "non-abused" siblings increase the probabilities of their own exploitation. There are many instances of multiple victims of incest or physical aggression within the same family. For a parent to exploit one child with impunity increases the likelihood of others in the family being hurt.

"THE STOCKHOLM SYNDROME"

One of the questions that perplexes many people is: Why do so many teenagers continue to endure incest and other severe parental abuse without resisting or escaping? This question is not unlike the question: Why do so many battered wives stay with their abusive husbands? One answer to both questions is to be found in understanding the "Stockholm Syndrome." The term "Stockholm Syndrome" was coined in the wake of a Swedish bank robbery where people were held hostage and terrorized for six days. What happened was that some of the hostages developed feelings of gratefulness, alliance, and even affection toward those who terrorized them. It is as if the victims were wearing blinders in that they overlooked the bad things done to them and instead, focused on apologies for their terrorists. This phenomenon occurs not only in terrorist-hostage situations, but also in more intimate relationships where parents abuse their children and husbands abuse their wives.

There are five conditions which form the basis of the Stockholm Syndrome:

1. The terrorist is seen by the victim as one who poses a severe threat to the victim's very survival.

2. The victim feels unable to escape from the terrorist.

3. The victim feels psychologically isolated from others who could be of assistance.

4. The terrorist manipulates the situation such that the victim is helpless and comes to be dependent on him or her to meet basic needs.

5. The terrorist displays a measure of "kindness" towards the victim, often in the context of meeting the victim's dependency needs.

This final condition—a display of "kindness"—is especially critical for it encourages the victim to deny the abuse and "bonds" the victim to the abuser. This dual process of denial and bonding is a means by which the victim can cope with a situation over which he or she has no control. Such "kindness" reinforces the victim's belief that the exploiter is "not really so bad," or that he will "change." It also helps to explain why some victims, even in the aftermath of horrendous exploitation, do not display anger toward their exploiter. It also explains why victims of sexual abuse, family violence, or peer exploitation do not leave the situation or report the abuse. Hence, what seems like self-destructive behavior from the outside is really a survival mechanism: the victim is in an untenable situation, responding reasonably to an unreasonable set of conditions which have been imposed upon him or her.

It should be emphasized that the term "syndrome" does not mean that the victim is responding in a pathological or abnormal manner. Rather, it is an understandable reaction given these conditions of terror, isolation, extreme dependency, and "kindness." It is also noteworthy that victimizers usually are very deliberate in creating these conditions. Users know how to manipulate in a way that increases their chances to continue exploiting while decreasing the risk of discovery. And the survival reactions of many victims, unfortunately, reinforce the victimizer's exploitive behavior.

THE "OH WOE IS ME" SYNDROME

There is one final characteristic that is common to victims which is both perplexing and tragic. This characteristic encompasses the feelings of insecurity, distrust, powerlessness and isolation already discussed. However, this characteristic appears, on the surface, to be the opposite of denial. It is what we refer to as the "Oh woe is me" syndrome. It is when victims of exploitation learn to see themselves as victims and then use this identity to manipulate others.

The "Oh woe is me" syndrome represents a **strategy** that some exploited people learn in order to help them cope with a terrible set of circumstances in their lives. When one has been a victim for a long period of time, it becomes increasingly difficult to deny to self and to others the harm that is done. Initially there may be denial. Yet attempts to deny repeated abuse become less convincing over time and do not alter the basic conditions of the abuse. For many teenage victims, there is a gradual realization that denying their hurt and confusion has not helped them. It is at this point that they may come to feel that admission of harm can be used as a tactic to gain some advantage.

Some victims of exploitation use what has happened to them as a tool to elicit attention, pity, or even special favors from others. They may also use what has befallen them as a convenient rationalization for their own inappropriate conduct toward others. Even well into adulthood, long after these victims have ceased to be harmed, the trauma of an earlier time is used as a justification for their actions. For some, it is a handy excuse for failing to change habits over which they have control–like being abusive parents or spouses.

The consequences are several. First, victims become so "fixated" with their having been victimized that in some respects their emotional growth and maturation is arrested. The abuse they endured seems to be a major focus for them in that it is frequently referred to on a daily basis. They may regularly bring it up in conversations, even when the topic of discussion appears to be unrelated. Even when others are "sick and tired" of hearing about it, some victims seem unable to refrain from making reference to their having been victimized.

Second, a related consequence of obsession with being a victim is that it drives people away, making an abused adolescent feel even more isolated and powerless. There comes a point in most relationships where others are no longer willing to accept another's victimization as an excuse for undesirable conduct. There is a feeling that the victim must take control of his or her life and no longer be defeated by events that happened in the past. There is also a sense of resentment when a victim continually uses being harmed as a means of gaining sympathy or attention.

The inevitable outcome is that those close to the victim begin to feel resentment rather than empathy. Their sympathy turns to anger and disgust. Indeed, they may even begin to withdraw, thus reinforcing the victim's feelings of distrust, isolation and lack of worth. While taking advantage of people's sympathy for them may temporarily help them cope, in the long run it is likely to add to their trauma. Abused teenagers must overcome any obsession with their victimization, just as others must try to understand the underlying reasons for the "Oh woe is me" syndrome.

THREE CONCLUSIONS

Three conclusions can be arrived at by studying the lives of abused teenagers. First, the undesirable emotional and behavioral problems of teenage victims of abusive parents emerge as consequences of their being victimized and are not the causes. Many people mistakenly believe that the misbehavior of teenage victims is what caused them to be harmed by others. The responsibility for being abused is misplaced on teenagers for problems which were, in the first place, caused by their having been abused and exploited.

Second, it is a mistake to assume that all abused teenagers will turn out as impaired adults. Some, if circumstances are favorable, will go into adulthood as relatively healthy individuals. Others will be hurt so badly that their mere survival is an accomplishment. It all depends upon what else happens to them.

Third, whether or not victims of parental abuse rise above the circumstances of their exploitation, there are certain common emotional and behavioral outcomes of abuse that are a burden for them. The burdens to be overcome are those feelings of denial, violation, insecurity, distrust, powerlessness, moral confusion, limited communication skills, psychological isolation, the "Stockholm Syndrome," and the "Oh woe is me" syndrome. All of these feelings are likely results of parents who use their children for their own selfish needs.

5

Exploitive Peers

Fist fights, verbal and physical harassment, malicious and demeaning "jokes," bullying, and acquaintance rape are all forms of abuse and exploitation. No one really knows how many young people regularly suffer at the hands of their peers. It is significant that when asked about the worst age in life, adults often cite their teenage years.

Furthermore, in every school, neighborhood or playground setting, one can find students who are victims of peer aggression. For some, it is subtle—for others, blatant. For all, it is odious. For victims of peer exploitation, every day constitutes a nearly unbearable pattern of hectoring, "minor" physical aggression, violations of rights, and other humiliations which are beyond their control. Among those who are abused by their peers, there is a fundamental sense of unpredictability and hostility wherever they go.

PEER AGGRESSION AND BULLYING

Sadly for many victims of peer abuse, there is no respite from their dehumanization. Perhaps the most remarkable feature of peer abuse is the silence. Victims, victimizers, and bystanders seldom reveal what is happening. However unpleasant, it is almost as if such abuses are accepted by teenagers as a "normal" part of growing up.

Furthermore, teenage victims seldom seek the help of adults. In fact, the involvement of parents, teachers, or other adults is likely to be resented. Rather than risk the humiliation of having to rely on adults, adolescent victims tend to endure any pain or degradation imposed by their peers. For victims to seek the help of an adult is perceived as an invitation to further misery; fear of reprisal helps keep them silent. Asking for help is an open admission of weakness, serving to reinforce one's status at the bottom of the pecking order.

Even the friends of victims are not likely to tell adults about what is happening. It is not that observers are necessarily complacent. Rather, their "conspiracy of silence" is in accordance with peer group norms which insulate youth from the "interference" of adult authority. Peers bear silent witness to these humiliations, helping to create a climate where bullying seems acceptable.

It is also noteworthy that fighting, bullying, hectoring and vandalism during adolescence are far more common among males than females. However, many women also learn to use physical violence against those weaker than themselves. An increasing number of young women are engaging in violent behavior. Like their male counterparts, some young women form gangs and pick on younger women or on a peer who is caught alone. As both males and females enter their adolescence, their abusiveness and exploitive behavior tends to increase.

Why does physical and emotional abusiveness increase with adolescence? Of course much, if not all, of such aggression is learned and rewarded. The "cult of machismo" has been dramatized in the make-believe world of television and films, and demonstrated in school, work, recreation, government, religion and family. It is clear that many males—and increasingly many females—learn from early on that aggression is expected and considered as normal. Its exercise can yield rewards. There are countless examples in which people are rewarded for their ability to exploit weaker or defenseless people.

While there may be community, peer and self controls on "excessive" abuse, such controls are least effective during the teenage years. This is especially true for those who have role models who are abusive people. Yet simply recognizing that the problem of exploitation and bullying involves learning does not fully explain why abuse occurs. What are some of the characteristics of abusive teenagers?

The most typical feature of adolescent abusers is that they have learned to have a very low sense of self-worth. For those low in self-esteem, physical and emotional aggressiveness are ways of compensating for feeling unimportant. For example, violence toward others is a way of gaining control, of feeling powerful, of being the center of attention. To be physically or verbally violent with impunity can temporarily diminish feelings of insecurity and powerlessness. By striking out at people weaker than themselves, abusive adolescents temporarily think of themselves as important.

Physical and emotional aggression occurs most often whenever people are consistently denied legitimate opportunities to feel respected. For them, aggression becomes a means of defense as well as a way to feel valued. In short, aggression is a way of using others for one's own gratification. Thus, selfishness or exploitation serves as a basis for much peer abuse. Young people, no less than adults, learn to be "users" of other people to gain a kind of respect. If peer aggression is to be reduced, then methods should involve helping young people find ways of acquiring feelings of self-worth through legitimate means.

Another feature of aggression has to do with the relative degree of excitement or stimulation present. Observers have long noted that human beings seek novelty, stimulation and change in their lives. Lacking excitement or challenge, humans become bored. Within the context of a non-stimulating, highly predictable environment, humans often seek to generate excitement, even if it means behaving in dangerously aggressive ways.

Many teenagers who are violent toward their peers define their settings as boring and predictable. To them, acting violently toward others is a way of generating excitement. Indeed, considerable energy can be directed toward being "creative" with respect to fighting and vandalism.

Violations of rules also create excitement and may even carry the added bonus of enhancing one's status with others. The risk-taking associated with "mindless vandalism," fighting, bullying, and other acts of violence by some teenagers, helps them to interject a degree of novelty into their environment. On the other hand, a constant state of violence loses its novelty. The price of abusive "entertainment" is therefore the need to increase the level of exploitation of others in order to be entertained. When one is entertained, one feels better. That is why many abusive young people find it so difficult to give up their aggressions. This can be seen in the case of bullying.

It is an unfortunate fact of life that bullies are present in nearly every school in the country. They represent a menace to untold thousands of their peers whose daily existence is reduced to fear, humiliation, revenge fantasies, and elaborate schemes of avoidance. Psychologist Dan Olweus, who has studied bullies for nearly two decades, estimates that approximately one in seven children is either a bully or is bullied. One in ten students is regularly the victim of harassment or attack by bullies. This translates into over five million bullied students every year in the U.S. and Canada alone. Consistent among the research on bullies are the following:

1. Male bullies are three to four times more likely than females to physically assault their victims. Females tend to be less direct in their form of bullying by ostracizing or shunning their victims. Young women have tended to use verbal harassment rather than physical attack as a means of domination. However, as we previously discussed, women are resorting to physical violence more and more.

2. Young people who are bullies tend to continue to exhibit serious antisocial patterns as adults unless there is therapy or other interventions. Young bullies have a one-in-four chance of acquiring a criminal record by age thirty. These bullies as adults also have more arrests for drunken driving, exhibit more abuse toward their spouses and children, and their occupational attainments are low as compared to others.

3. Bullies are most often reared in homes conducive to the
    development of aggression.   These homes exhibit parental
    violence,   extensive   use   of   physical   punishment,
    inconsistencies in discipline, poor communication between
    family members, limited parental monitoring of the child,
    and limited skills regarding family problem-solving. As a
    case in point, consider the story of "Itchy."

Our Bully: Itchy

"We called him 'Itchy' which seemed appropriate because
of the effect he had on his victims. He was like a bad case of
poison ivy for which there was no relief. But we didn't think
of that at the time.   All we knew was that Itchy meant
trouble. He was mean, vindictive, and self-centered.

"Itchy would go to great lengths to taunt the other kids.
He seemed to delight in selecting someone smaller than him,
slapping a KICK ME sign on a kid's back, and smile with glee
as he booted him down the corridor.   Sabotaging lockers,
stealing pens and other small objects, and pushing his way into
line were routine.   He even seemed to specialize in grabbing
someone's lunch and throwing it with great force against the
ground.

"Itchy was always very good at making it seem as if his
victims deserved to be the objects of derision.   He was
creative at inventing some provocation which justified his tor-
ments.   Any weakness, however insignificant, could generate
from him torrents of invective.   He was relentless and totally
without mercy.

"Itchy also loved an audience.   He was an absolute master
at creating situations were onlookers would be too intimated to
intervene. He thus gained from his observers what he felt was
their approval.   He enjoyed the attention, he enjoyed the

control he exerted over others, and saddest of all, he enjoyed seeing his victims in pain. For Itchy, dominating and humiliating others was a source of entertainment.

"The last time I saw Itchy was at a class reunion, many years after high school graduation. He was drunk and very loud. He was alone; apparently he had been divorced several times. There were rumors that he had been in trouble with the law. Classmates at the reunion were avoiding him. Although Itchy was older, he did not appear any wiser. But now I felt differently: instead of hating Itchy, I felt sorry for him." (Name withheld.)

There is some debate whether or not bullies exhibit low self-esteem. Some argue that bullies are not insecure because they feel superior to their victims. Others contend that bullies are indeed insecure but are so hardened that their insecurity is difficult to detect.

It is possible that both arguments are partially correct. Because many bullies come from abusive or troubled homes, it is likely that they experience fundamental insecurities and low self-esteem.

Bullying may be learned as an adaptive response to feelings of insecurity and low self-esteem acquired from a troubled home life. By bullying, one can temporarily feel powerful and important, feel superior to others, and be the center of attention. Bullying creates fleeting moments of feeling good about oneself, without altering the fundamental conditions which produce such noxious behavior. In this sense, bullying is a way of compensating for low self-esteem in other situations, particularly home life.

Victims often exhibit very poor self-images in regard to being able to deal with bullies. Those who are victimized are nearly always physically weaker than those who prey upon them. Victims may feel insecure, anxious, unattractive and stupid. Many are social isolates, but not all are. They may deviate from the norms of their peers in terms of dress codes, the social skills required of the street, and in their intellectual achievements. While a minority of victims engage in provocative acts which "require" a response from a bully, the majority are passive individuals who unwittingly become scapegoats for bullies. Being bullied has the unfortunate consequence of exacerbating a victim's feelings of worthlessness, and of being weak and alone.

While no one suggests that victims have a need to be bullied, their vulnerabilities are readily detected and exploited by their predatory peers. Once the bullying starts, these victims spend their teenage years in virtually a constant state of anxiety, avoiding certain places, perhaps missing school days, and in the extreme, contemplating or attempting suicide.

What has been described so far is exploitation by both young men and women. However, there is one other area of violence in which women are almost always the victims, and that is in the area of date rape.

DATE RAPE

During the teenage years, females are at the highest risk of being sexually assaulted. Over 57% of all reported rape victims are between twelve and nineteen years of age, and conservative estimates are that over a quarter of a million female and male teenagers will be raped each year in the United States and Canada. Millions more risk the probability of being raped. Although statistics vary, the best estimates suggest that well over one-half of all of these rape victims are attacked by someone who is known and trusted. In a great many cases, rape occurs in the context of a dating situation where the victim is in her teens. Sexual assault by someone who is known and trusted can be just as devastating as rape by a stranger; oftentimes, more so.

According to one recent study of teenage females, approximately twenty percent had been physically forced by a date to have sexual intercourse. Nearly one-half said they had been touched, held or kissed against their will. Other studies also report high percentages of rape, attempted rape, and other forms of sexual assault and physical violence being inflicted on young women by their male acquaintances.

However, while acquaintance rape is common, it should be emphasized that most young women are **not** raped and most young men are **not** rapists. Indeed, the vast majority of teenagers experience dating relationships with neither serious incident nor injury. Yet, there exists common misunderstandings in society concerning sexual rights and the meaning of consent. People still mistakenly believe that rape only occurs when physical force is used, yet fail to realize that threat, deception and psychological manipulation are also used in attacks.

To further aggravate the situation, most males think of rape as only a problem for females. Males are raped too. Also, most males fail to grasp the role they play in influencing the recovery of victims. It is, therefore, important to help all males, as well as females, understand what is involved in acquaintance rape and how they should respond.

If males are not taught the implications of their actions, victims of date rape are often left with lingering feelings that they are somehow at fault. Unfortunately, too many victims are mistakenly made to feel guilty for using poor judgment or for failing to control some male's "natural urges." Little wonder that many victims of acquaintance rape experience confusion, guilt and long term emotional problems. Many contemplate or attempt suicide. And since victims of acquaintance rape are unlikely to seek help from those who can minister to their needs, their trauma is sharpened; little comfort is gained and they suffer in silence.

The confusion among teenage victims and their unwillingness to seek help stems from widely held beliefs that after a certain   degree of kissing and petting, males have sexual rights, regardless of a female's objections. It is common in dating situations for a teenager to want to make a favorable impression by showing she is friendly, trusting, sexually attractive and accepting.   Yet some males interpret such friendliness and good will as an indication of desire for sexual intimacy.

As the male makes advances, she may try gently to discourage him in order to spare his feelings. While most males do **not** go beyond the boundaries set by women, for some, "no" means "yes."   This is especially true if there has been prior intimacy such as heavy kissing.   The end result may be that her trust is used against her as he forces his demands on her or manipulates her into a compromising situation.   Thus, an unfair burden is placed on females to recognize when males can no longer control their "urges."

This false and dangerous view presumes that each female is responsible for any male's aggressiveness or lack of control. However, we should all understand that females do not "trigger" rape; the source of rape is always the rapist.   The basic source of any rape of an acquaintance is not a sexual need.   The basic source is a selfishness on the part of the rapist. The rapist, whether an acquaintance or a stranger, is willing to use someone else for his own needs without regard for the needs or rights of others. Exploitation, in other words, is a basic aspect of every rape. Some acquaintances may use rape to fulfill their particular sexual and other desires. Others may rape to demonstrate power to self or others. Whatever the case, acquaintance rape is the ultimate in being a selfish user of another person.

HOW DOES DATE RAPE OCCUR?

Date rape is not usually a sudden assault without warning. There are often a number of cues given off by rapists which indicate the possibility of attack, but which victims may not interpret as signs. The attacker acts subtly, positioning himself through a gradual series of encroachments.

First, there are "minor" invasions of the intended victim's physical and psychological space. These include gratuitous and unwanted touching, and persistently discussing topics with sexual themes. Remarks about one's appearance or anatomy, about the appearance or anatomy of others, frequent references to being "sexy," or constantly seeking opportunities to be in close physical proximity with the intended victim are common tactics.

Although the potential victim initially is uncomfortable with these invasions, she eventually gets used to them. The sheer persistence of intrusion results in her letting her guard down. The intended victim may feel ". . . that's just the way he is." The conduct is seen as normal, even though it may be escalating in frequency and intensity. She is thus desensitized to the potential threat.

Finally, the rapist seeks an opportunity to get the victim alone and in a situation where she feels safe. Her "consenting" to be with him makes her more easily comprised. Unwittingly she may, through her trust, make it easier for him to rape her. Her trust in him is turned against her as she is blamed for "inviting" the attack.

The male is likely to deny that he assaulted the victim, implying that she gave consent to a sexual interlude. His denials add to her feelings of confusion and guilt, and reinforce the belief among others that she is responsible.

A common myth, sometimes promoted among males, is that those who are raped enjoy the experience. This is merely a rationalization to deny the exploitive nature of rape. Rape is a violent, traumatic, and degrading act that females and males who are raped neither desire nor enjoy. Rape is **not** the same as "making love"; it is a violation of one's right to control one's body and of one's ability to make a sexual choice. No one ever has the right to impose such a situation on another. People who sexually exploit others bear the responsibility, not their victims. It is both inappropriate and harmful to suggest to any victim of rape, whether by a stranger or by a trusted acquaintance, that she "asked for it" or "deserved" what has happened.

Such deeply felt confusion over the victim's judgment and responsibility is intensified by mutual friends when they claim that "he's not that kind of guy." In other cases, the victim will be cut off from the support of family and friends because she remained silent for fear of not being believed. The victim may feel that family and peers will claim that she provoked the rapist and invited the attack. No one wants to be unjustly cast in the role of "provocateur."

There are other ways in which the effects of acquaintance rape on a victim are different from those of rape by a total stranger. When a teenager is raped by a total stranger, family and friends are likely to believe that she is a victim, and they will try to be supportive. If the rape took place during a dating situation, however, family and friends may doubt her and unintentionally withhold their support.

When the rapist operates in the same social circle as the victim and others close to her, there are very serious complications. The rapist may be at the same school or place of work as the victim. This means that some people who know both the victim and her assailant will "take sides." Some will be against the victim, who will then become the object of gossip, rumor, and ridicule. Worst of all is when the victim must cross paths with her assailant.

To the extent that the rapist has friends and communication links within the same social network as his victim, the victim's potential support system is undermined and her version of events is called into question. Such a situation makes recovery very difficult to achieve.

Not only is a victim sometimes doubted by others, but she may be accused of "making up stories" and that she agreed to sexual intercourse. People may believe that the victim was being a "tease" or "led the rapist on" and therefore deserved what happened. Even police officers sometimes dismiss cases of date rape as simply "lovers' quarrels," or as attempts to seek revenge. One result of this lack of credibility is that rape victims are made to feel alone and without support. Worse, they are made to feel guilty at a time when they most need the support and understanding of others.

Being raped by a date undermines a victim's ability to trust others. Victims learn to doubt their ability to judge the character of others and begin to feel unsure of themselves, even around their friends. They may become so uncertain that they withdraw from former friends and feel unsafe even in familiar settings.

A victim's lack of faith in her ability to judge the character of others, combined with feelings of apprehension, usually lasts for a long time—even years. Unfortunately, such feelings may develop into a generalized distrust of all men, including those who deserve trust, and who would otherwise be good friends.

Finally, one of the most unfortunate consequences of date rape is that it heightens fears about human intimacy, especially sexual intimacy. The ability to trust others and to share with them on an emotional and on a physical level is basic to human happiness. To be the cause of undermining the capacity in others to love, to trust, and to share is to have inflicted great injury on them.

Part of the problem of date rape among teenagers can be attributed to the tremendous pressure adolescents impose on each other. In the face of pressure to date, coupled with the desire for acceptance, many teenagers unwittingly find themselves compromised and manipulated. It is difficult for many, especially those with little experience, to recognize situations that can progress into crises. It is likewise difficult for many young women to be assertive with particularly aggressive men. For those teenagers who are victimized, there is fear that their rape will be revealed and they will suffer shame.

On a positive note, several things are happening to make life somewhat better for rape victims. Rape crisis centers are now in many towns and cities. They are serving their communities by providing counseling and other services. Anyone who is raped, or any parent or friend of a rape victim, should seek out the help of the nearest rape crisis center. Also, authorities are becoming more responsive. The courts are increasingly treating rape and other forms of violence inflicted by peers as serious offenses. They are also giving more credence to the testimony of teenagers than was true in the past. Similarly, some police departments are now receiving training in working with rape victims. They are learning that acquaintance rape is not a "lovers' quarrel." However, prosecutors are clearly in need of public pressure to treat date rape as rape. Prosecutors decide who goes to trial, and no one can expect justice without their cooperation.

Given current trends in schools and colleges, a strong positive concern is emerging for reducing the rape of young women. Schools and colleges are beginning to provide valuable information to students and teachers. In recent years, teachers have been sought out and have learned about their roles in regard to assuring the rights and responsibilities of young people. More and more, parents are learning to be understanding and non-judgmental toward their children if they have suffered rape. However, much remains to be learned and practiced by everyone——authorities, parents, educators and teenagers—in order to reduce the probabilities of date rape as a hideous form of exploitation.

6

Substance Abuse

The abuse of alcohol and other drugs constitutes one of the most serious health and social risks confronting adolescents. Although not a new phenomenon, the volume of media coverage demonstrates a growing awareness of the drug problem. Nearly everyone agrees that the cost of substance abuse to teenagers, their families, communities, and to society is enormous. There is also agreement that vast numbers of youth are abusing drugs and alcohol. However, there is no clear consensus on its causes and there is no agreement on the best approach to reduce substance abuse.

Yet, there is at least one source from which virtually all forms of substance abuse among teenagers arise: the peer subculture. The sad fact is that drug subcultures are pervasive in most junior and senior high schools. It is the exception rather than the rule for a student body to be completely drug free. Drug usage is so common in most schools that many students, even those who do not use illicit substances, view consumption of drugs and alcohol among peers as a regular part of school life.

PROFILE OF TEENAGE DRUG USE

- Nearly one-third of high school seniors report getting drunk abut once per week; five percent report drinking alcohol daily.

- The National Institute on Drug Abuse reports that 40% of seniors have used drugs other than marijuana; 55% have used marijuana.

- Before the upsurge in the use of "crack," 17% of seniors had tried cocaine at least once; current estimates are that over a quarter of the teenage population has experimented with cocaine.

- About 1% of seniors have used heroine.

- One in five seniors smokes cigarettes daily.

- 85% of seniors indicate that it is relatively easy for them to acquire marijuana.

- 40% of teenagers identify drug abuse as the leading problem facing their generation.

- One should not confuse a drop in drug use in one area with a drop in overall drug use. For example, marijuana usage may drop while alcohol usage or cocaine usage may increase. Drug use is very faddish and subject to fluctuation. Overall, the pattern has been and continues to be an increase in chemical usage by teenagers.

PEER GROUP SUPPORTS

Peer groups represent powerful forces in the lives of adolescents. Studies of high school youth indicate that teenagers often experience conflict when having to choose between their friends and their parents. The peer group is especially critical with respect to a teenager's decision to use drugs or alcohol.

Peer pressure to drink and to experiment with illicit drugs increases as one enters adolescence. Moreover, many teenagers do not grant credibility to adult warnings about drugs. In addition, teenagers often avoid surveillance by adults. As a result, they have some freedom to experiment with drug lifestyles in peer group settings. Likewise, many perceive few risks as a consequence of drug experimentation. Indeed, teenagers often see it as a badge of independence to flirt with various "deviant" activities such as smoking, drinking alcohol, or the consumption of illicit drugs.

In the early stages of experimentation, drugs are not used to "escape" or to kill pain. Rather, drug and alcohol use at this stage is more a rite of passage from the dependency of childhood into what is thought of as adulthood. Furthermore, use of illicit substances is one means of gaining status and acceptance among certain groups of peers within the school and neighborhood. For many, drug experimentation is a way of establishing friends and of developing and testing one's emerging social skills.

Moreover, because drug users are engaged in an activity which departs from both legal codes and from mainstream adult values, the "hidden and forbidden" character of users holds a mysterious fascination for many teenagers. Many take pride in their ability to get away with drug use, to flaunt convention and to consume something that is considered taboo. They feel superior to others because of their ability to use drugs. For them, substance abuse is a means of achieving a sense of uniqueness. It gives them a feeling of being creative, especially if other means of creative expression are thwarted.

Drinking and other drug use can also create illusions of power and competency. For those with weak feelings of confidence, such substance use can be seen as valuable in overcoming a sense of inadequacy. All of these beliefs and feelings regarding the benefits of drugs and alcohol are reinforced by peers who are users.

Where drugs are used by groups to recruit and retain new group members, the power of the group is enhanced by the fact that drugs are illegal. It requires being organized and secretive, thus giving the group considerable influence over new recruits. When one uses illicit drugs extensively to become an accepted member, it is difficult to escape the group's influence. Further compounding the problem is the fact that once adolescents move from occasional attempts at experimentation to the development of habits of drug use, non-users will care less to associate with them. Likewise, the user may cease to seek the company of non-users. As a result, increasing numbers of the experimenter's new friends will be drug users. When youngsters share illegal drugs, they are sharing danger and the thrill of conspiracy. This sharing creates a strong bond among them. Drug-using groups thereby reinforce in their new members habits of drug and alcohol abuse, which in turn strengthen their ties to the drug using community.

Of course, a drug-using peer group may not represent a safe haven or a bastion of support. While it is true that peers can offer a sense of belonging, it is also true that they are often a source of exploitation. Even among so called "close friends," principles of friendship such as caring and trust are often violated.   Studies indicate that a large proportion of teenagers say they have been hurt by their friends and often describe their closest friends as being distrustful and selfish.

Even when friends do not mean to hurt their friends, they can.   Oftentimes, drug-abusing peers will be unintentionally exploitive when they are trying to be accepting of a friend. For example, initiating the novice into the "joys" of drugs and alcohol, is not beneficial and is risky.   However, a successful initiation reaffirms the power of the group over the individual, as well as being a source of great amusement for the more drug experienced members.   Simply stated, it is "fun" to watch a novice "get loaded."   This is the price of group acceptance by the new member.   Thus, the group benefits in entertainment despite the costs to the new member.   This is an exploitive yet common way that drug usage begins.

To consider the importance of peer networks is not to minimize the significance of other conditions related to drug and alcohol consumption.   For instance, parental use of alcohol and drugs is related to teenage use.   Children of alcoholics have a very high probability of developing into alcoholics when compared to children of nonalcoholics.   Nevertheless, the one condition common to nearly all substance abuse is the influence of peer groups.

Teenagers often consume alcohol or drugs because they do not wish to stand out as different from their peers.   Collective consumption of illicit drugs entrenches the individual with the group and promotes feelings of security and trust through the sharing of secret "underground" activities.   To dramatize the importance of the "peer underground" of users, consider the specifics of the learning process that a typical adolescent experiences in developing a habit of substance abuse.

To begin, the teenager must know someone who is a user who will provide the drugs.   During the first several episodes, the novice is taught how to acquire drugs, how to consume them properly in correct amounts, how to recognize the stages of becoming "high," how to avoid detection, and ultimately how to enjoy the experience. This entire process transpires in a setting where the novice is in the company of people who seem to be friends and where the potential dangers are made to seem minimal or nonexistent. "Side effects" such as feeling sick and disoriented are defined as a small price to pay for the advantages of getting high. The illegal nature of drug use is trivialized. The activity is pictured as merely another form of recreation. Refusal to partake in this activity is tantamount to cowardice.

A rule among many adolescents, including nonusers, is one of noninterference. Most young people know who the regular users are in their school or neighborhood, and nearly every teenager can identify someone who has at least tried an illicit substance. Thus, there is either open support for drug and alcohol consumption, or at least there is little likelihood that peers will intervene by telling adults. If anything, there is a tacit agreement not to inform on users, or even to try to discourage them. In fact, many teenagers do not think that adults should be concerned with whether they or other teenagers consume alcohol or other drugs. Thus, there is a tacit "conspiracy" among adolescents to keep adults uninformed of drug use. This "conspiracy" is part of most adolescent norms which encourage emancipation from the controls of parents and other adults.

In summary, adolescent peer groups provide both the means and the justification for the consumption of alcohol and drugs. While not every teenager becomes a substance abuser, drug and alcohol use is so common that often it ceases to be noteworthy among users and nonusers alike. The friendship networks that are established among users, the role models provided by peers, the need to demonstrate independence, the values of noninterference prevalent among adolescents, and the natural curiosity about an outlaw activity that has received so much attention combine to produce a compelling pressure on adolescents to become involved in drug and alcohol consumption.

There are vast differences among peer groups, and it would be unreasonable to imply that all teenage subcultures are alike. Within every school or neighborhood, there exists a broad spectrum of cliques among the teenage population. However, an interesting feature of adolescent substance abuse is that it is not limited to a particular racial or social group. There are athletic cliques using drugs, there are academic cliques using drugs, and there are relatively conforming and relatively delinquent groups using drugs. Among teenagers, substance abuse may be the one factor which truly touches the entire spectrum of peer groups.

It is difficult for many adults to understand why some students from wealthier families sell illicit drugs. They certainly do not need the income. It is easier to rationalize a reason for poor people selling drugs than wealthy people. The poor, it is said, need money more than do children from more affluent backgrounds. However, in neither case does financial gain adequately explain most teenage drug "dealing." It may explain some adult drug dealers, but adolescents often have a more primary motive than financial reward.

The selling of illicit drugs is a means of gaining additional prestige. They not only sell drugs, they often give drugs away. These young drug dealers thereby become a focal point of attention and sometimes honor from their peers. They also feel like they have power. Unfortunately, many young people look up to their peer drug suppliers.

Ironically, it is not merely the socially isolated adolescent who becomes involved in substance abuse as a means of gaining peer acceptance. Young people who are well integrated into various community and friendship peer networks are also at risk of developing drug and alcohol abuse patterns. The great majority of youngsters will be exposed to considerable pressure to consume illicit substances at some point during their teenage years.

WHY DO THEY DO IT?

Drug and Alcohol Abuse Among Teenagers Provides:

- a means to achieve prestige;

- a way to demonstrate independence;

- a basis for sharing and cooperating with peers;

- a feeling of compensation when individual expression and creativity are perceived to have been thwarted;

- a means to dull the pain of failures experienced at home, school or elsewhere;

- a sense of security with peers;

- a temporary feeling of power, of being able to manipulate events and of creating outcomes with impunity; and

- a feeling of acceptance and attention when drugs and alcohol are shared.

Taken together, the above functions of drug and alcohol consumption can work in concert to temporarily enhance feelings of self-importance. Drug and alcohol consumption becomes even more important to those teenagers who have little opportunity to feel good about themselves in other ways.

However, whatever the individual psychological reasons for using drugs, the primary source is exploitation. Exploitation panders to the psychological weaknesses of others. Parents or peers who are "users" of their children or friends, foster substance abuse as surely as they do running away and suicide.

7

Running Away

Thousands of teenagers in the United States and Canada are "urban nomads" who live like hardened adults on the streets of large cities. They are like veterans of guerrilla combat who learn to survive by whatever means necessary. Their life on the streets is one of exploiting and being exploited. The personal and social costs of running away are huge, especially with regard to the spread of disease.

RUNAWAYS AND DISEASE

Because there are several hundred thousand runaways involved in prostitution and drug trafficking, some believe these adolescents will become the third wave of the AIDS epidemic. As noted by Patricia Hersch, in the January 1988 issue of Psychology Today, "there may never be an actual epidemic among adolescents because the latency period between infection and appearance of symptoms may be ten years or longer." For many years, they will likely engage in sexual exploration with friends and with those who pay for their services. They will have ample opportunity to acquire and spread the disease because prostitution and drug trafficking are about the only ways that adolescents can survive on the streets. Because they are the sexual targets of many who have AIDS, runaways will spread the disease rapidly.

Runaways tend not to take precautions regarding their own health or the spread of disease to others. Practicing "safe-sex" is not likely for most teenagers because:

1) they tend to live for the here and now—ten years from now is meaningless to most adolescents;

2) they are migratory, moving from one urban area to another;

3) they are generally ignorant of the character of AIDS; and

4) their bodies—both young men and young women are likely to be exhausted, chronically ill, and stressed out.

THEIR REASONS

Why are so many running away today? How many are running? In 1984, the Department of Health and Human Services estimated that there were between 730,000 and 1.3 million runaways of whom about 500,000 were permanently homeless. More conservative estimates place the number of permanently homeless at about 300,000.

Approximately two out of three runaways are spontaneous responses to a conflict with their parents or peers. They tend to leave without making any provisions for survival. More than half of all runaways leave home with nothing but the clothes they are wearing and have no clear idea of where they will go. Even if the decision to leave is not spontaneous, the overwhelming majority of teenage runaways are leaving behind a seriously troubled home life.

Although many runaways do not leave their home towns and may try to stay with relatives or friends, many travel considerable distances from home and encounter great risks of being victimized. Indeed, the probability of being physically harmed, sexually assaulted or drawn into illegal activities is high among nearly all runaways.

Despite the fact that shelter houses for runaways exist in many cities and towns, the vast majority of runaways do not go to them. They sleep in bus stations, railway stations, parks, empty buildings, or worse, they locate streetwise persons who seemingly "befriend" them but then exploit them. As a consequence of their new relationships they are often sexually used, forced into prostitution, seduced into drug use and drug dealing, involved in theft or in other ways victimized. The longer the runaway's period of absence from home, the greater the risk of involvement in illegal activities. About twenty percent of all runaways end up in court as a result of delinquent behavior. Nearly all engage in behavior which would result in court action if they were caught.

There are other obvious consequences of running away. Youth who leave have their schooling halted and many never return. Their health tends to suffer at a time that is critical to their development. Malnutrition and chronic infections are common. Runaways also are at a distinct disadvantage in finding legitimate work that will sustain them, let alone provide the life styles they have learned to value. Crime for some runaways becomes their only apparent solution.

However, most runaways are not delinquents before they leave home. Neither are most runaways mentally ill. Running away for some teenagers is a rational act regardless of the risks because they are in immediate danger at home. From their perspective, running may be the only sensible thing for them to do. A number of undesirable conditions, such as severe physical and sexual abuse at home, make running seem to be a reasonable course of action. Running away also seems to be a viable option for many because of how they think authorities will respond to their charges of parental abuse. They may believe that by reporting on their parents they will be in even more danger than if they live on the streets.

In other cases, youngsters feel forced to run away by the choices imposed upon them. For example, many young runaways feel that they were forced to choose between their parents and their boy- or girlfriends. Other teenagers leave because of dreams of achieving fame and glory, and others merely seek adventure. A consideration of the three main categories of youths who leave home will provide an understanding of the wide variety of motivations and situations that characterize runaways.

CATEGORY I: TRUE RUNAWAYS

The first and by far the largest group of runaways (estimates ranging from 75% to 90%) are those who are seriously distraught over conditions at home or with their peers. Members of this group seek to flee because of feeling that they are abused, rejected or exploited. Unhappiness over their situations, plus the desire to gain more control over their lives, are their primary reasons for fleeing. They tend to leave home with little regard for any consequences. For them, nothing that could happen elsewhere could be worse than the dangerous or inhibiting lives they feel they are enduring at home or with their peers.

For some of these teenagers, there is the added expectation that by running away they will punish their parents or others. They hope to make them feel sorry. In other words, running away can be both an act of escape and an act of punishment. It is also a way of dramatically calling attention to conditions which they think are intolerable.

Yet running away does not end the misery they experience. Most youth who run have no clear idea of the difficulties of living a life on the streets. Some have a very romanticized view of "being free." Others simply do not understand the kinds of exploitation and harm they are likely to encounter if they seek "refuge" in a dangerous and chaotic urban area. These youth do not realize the risks nor do they realize their own vulnerabilities.

In a very real sense, runaways are caught in a no-win situation: life at home is viewed as intolerable, and life on the streets is beset with pain and trouble. Nonetheless, most of them choose to return home, often as a result of a friend's or relative's encouragement. Some are located and returned by authorities and agencies. Yet, returning home does not usually result in a resolution of the problems that induced them to run away in the first place. They tend to run away from home many times.
Certainly, many parents are shocked by their child's having run away and, given a second chance, work effectively to improve relations between themselves and their children.

Unfortunately, an even more common reaction is for the parents to punish their child for the discomfort he or she is perceived to have precipitated. Frequently, these parents experience intensified feelings of anger and rejection, and act in ways to "get even" or to "teach their teenager a lesson." As a result, they make worse the very problems that resulted in their child's running away in the first place.

Responding to runaways as if they are "sick," "strange," "hostile," or "delinquent" only serves to further isolate them when they have the greatest need for support. Usually, parental attempts to punish or stigmatize teenagers for running away only worsens the teenager's self-image and intensifies feelings of rejection. It also makes it difficult for teenagers who return home to behave in ways desired by their parents.

Given that many runaways feel isolated from their families, the school is perhaps the only institution where feelings of belonging and a sense of commitment can be fostered. Involvement in extracurricular activities, opportunities to feel successful in school work or in peer relations, and the feeling of being in control of one's environment can and should be developed among runaways within the school setting. Indeed, creating a "place of acceptance" is perhaps the only remedy to the problem of youth who choose the streets as a way of coping with their pain.

Among the most common warning signals associated with running away are frequent and intense battles with parents concerning the teenager's emerging independence. Parental objections to dating partners, the selection of friends, keeping late hours, the lack of assuming responsibilities at home, and the presence of school-related problems which result in threats about leaving should be taken seriously.

CATEGORY II: POSITIVE RUNAWAYS

A second category of runaways are those who are termed "positive" runaways. They are running toward a new situation rather than away from troubles at home or school. For example, they may be running away to get married, join the army, or find employment. They have little dislike for their home life. In fact, they often feel very guilty for having run away. They tend to be older, ages 16 or 17, and they are seeking adventure, romance, or work. They tend to have an idyllic view of the world and depart in a quest of discovery. In our estimation, the number of "positive" runaways is a small proportion of the total number who leave home. Many of these runaways return home within a short period of time after experiencing the adverse realities of life on the streets.

CATEGORY III: "KICK OUTS"

There is another small group of runaways consisting of those young people who are not really running away. Rather, they are forced to "get out" of their homes. They are ordered to leave, are disowned or are abandoned. Typically this group is neither reported to authorities by parents or others, nor do these youngsters seek to return home. These youth are truly "pushouts." They would be in a dangerous situation if not "pushed out" and their lives are made dangerous if pushed out. This group has the worst time of finding a decent survival.

IF A TEENAGER RUNS AWAY: SUGGESTIONS FOR PARENTS

Many parents are shocked and dismayed to learn that

their son or daughter has run away. The following are suggestions for parents to follow if they discover their child has unexpectedly left home.

• Do not delay in contacting the police. Many police departments do not act on missing persons reports for at least 24 hours after being notified. Be persistent in requesting that they take prompt action. Provide police with a recent photograph of the teenager, medical and dental records, fingerprints or other appropriate physical evidence.

• Contact the child's friends to find out where he or she might have gone, who saw the child last, or if there were any "secrets" the child may have divulged to friends.

• Contact national organizations for help. For example, the National Runaway Switchboard (800-621-4000) allows children and parents to leave messages for one another. Other organizations include the National Network of Runaway and Youth Services (800-HIT-HOME), Child Find (800-431-5005), and Covenant House (800-999-9999). Also, make sure the police contact the nearest FBI office regarding your missing child.

• Contact all relatives who may be sought out by the runaway youth. This may include a natural parent who lives separately due to divorce, former stepparents or surrogate parents who lived with the child, aunts, uncles, and grandparents of the youth, or anyone else known to have had a primary relationship with him or her. Runaway youth often contact or visit persons with whom they have had a significant relationship at some point in their lives.

• If you manage to contact your runaway child, avoid the

tendency to argue or blame him or her, or to threaten punishment if he or she returns home. Tell your child that he or she is loved and together you will solve any problems.

WARNING SIGNS

In the heat of an argument, a parent and teenager may each psychologically reject the other. Under such circumstances, the likelihood for the occurrence of verbal and physical violence is high. Indeed, frequent and intense arguments with parents appear to be the precipitating events in approximately half of all runaway cases. Intense conflicts with a stepparent or live-in parent surrogate are especially common among these runaways.

Another condition that signals the possibility of a teenager's running away is a parent's indifference to his or her child's problems. Such indifference can be expressed in several ways. However said, an "I don't care" attitude toward one's child often sets the stage for the child to leave home. More directly, some parents cause their children to leave home by constantly saying that their children are burdens; that their children cause them to make too many sacrifices. To be sure, when parents do not value their children, their children are likely to be linked with delinquency, troubles at school, and conflicts at home——all of which are associated with running away.

Whenever one recognizes a history of social and psychological degradation of a teenager, one is observing an important precondition for running away. Many runaway youth feel that their parents "hate them" or that they are being singled out as family scapegoats. A pattern of child abuse, violence between parents, fear of parental punishment, and sibling hatred are also family conditions which increase the probabilities of running away. Not surprisingly, parental alcoholism is associated with the patterns of neglect and abuse that set the stage for many departures. In the majority of cases where a teenager is running from a troubled home life, the problem at home appears to be chronic and long-term rather than sudden.

Teenagers are likely to run away not only because of precipitating incidents at home, but also because of other difficulties. Parents may not be fully aware of these other problems because their children are hiding them. They may feel unable to discuss them openly out of fear of punishment or condemnation. It is not uncommon for pregnant teenagers to run away from home because they do not want their parents to discover their condition. Youth in trouble with the law or who are having homosexual experiences also may leave home rather than face their parents.

Feeling that conditions are intolerable at school, work, or with peers can also contribute to running away. Youths who are constantly ridiculed and tormented by their peers, or who are continually criticized or stigmatized at school, may seek to free themselves from such rejection and humiliation. Frequent truancy, fights, academic failure, non-participation in desired school activities, and frequent suspension are all behaviors associated with running away.

Persistent feelings of loneliness, depression, failure, and low self-esteem, when compounded and reinforced with problems at home or with friends, also increase the likelihood of running away. Obviously, recognizing the presence of these conditions should serve as warnings that teenagers may seek to run away or, worse, may attempt suicide (the ultimate in running away.) Those who have close friends who have "solved" problems by running away, or those who have made previous attempts at running away or suicide, are at especially high risk.

After their children run away, parents often recognize that their children gave them many cues that they would leave home. However, most parents fail to heed such warnings in time. In fact, it comes as a shock to most parents. Even when their children associate with peers who have run away, many parents fail to anticipate the possibility that their own child will depart. However, seldom does a teenager leave home without giving strong hints to family and friends. Unfortunately, these cues seldom receive a response before the drastic action of running is taken. The result of the departure is that the life chances for most runaways are made worse.

While undesirable home conditions are the cause of many runaways, children also run away from healthy home environments. In such cases, there is usually a conflict between the values of the parents and those of the youth's peer culture. Western culture is very youth oriented and promotes values of early sexual freedom, lavish consumption, quick fix solutions, and early automony for young people that are unrealistic. Thus, it is not an easy task for families to foster in their children the desire to remain at home when their children are taught to feel the need to leave in order to attain the rights they think are due them.

Nevertheless, having a healthy home life and feeling a sense of accomplishment and belonging at school are the best deterrents to running away. At the very least, knowing how to identify the signs of crisis and knowing how to find help for teenagers at risk are critical skills for parents and school personnel to develop in order to prevent such drastic action as running away.

8

Suicide

A teenager does not have to leave home in order to run away. The ultimate and most tragic form of running away is suicide. Suicide is the second leading cause of death among teenagers. By some estimates, as many as twenty-five percent of teenagers have suicidal thoughts at some point during adolescence. The American Association of Suicidology conservatively estimates that the current rate of attempted suicide ranges between forty-eight and sixty thousand young people each year. Other estimates are as high as four-hundred thousand. One thing is certain: during the past two decades, the adolescent suicide rate has more than doubled.

WHY SUICIDE?

As one might expect, many of the chronic problems associated with running away are also key factors in adolescent suicide. Typically, the suicidal teenager is experiencing problems at home or in school which result in a variety of acting-out behaviors. Alcohol or drug abuse, running away, loss of interest in usually pleasurable activities, withdrawal from interactions with friends, belligerence toward authority figures, a disregard for personal appearance or safety, emotional outbursts, giving away treasured items, and other forms of acting-out are indicative of the kinds of turmoil that precede suicide. The death of a family member or close friend is another condition that precedes some suicides. A "psychotic break" or fear of "going crazy" is also a precipitating factor in some cases. However, the most common feature of a suicide-prone person, is severe and continuous depression. The most common feature of non-physically or chemically induced depression is living in an exploitive situation where one's identity is meaningless beyond serving the needs of others. Exploitive people can subtly induce suicide in others.

Adolescents who contemplate suicide usually experience intense feelings of sadness, worthlessness, isolation and power-lessness. These feelings seem to dominate their lives. Oftentimes they communicate their suicidal thoughts to trusted friends in statements such as "no one really cares about me, so what's the point of living," or "sometimes dying seems easier than living." Unfortunately, feelings of worthlessness and isolation are likely to be reinforced when others fail to take such statements seriously.

These feelings experienced by teenagers may seem quite unlikely from the "objective" perspective of others. Indeed, parents and friends of suicide prone adolescents may focus on aspects of the teenager's life which have little to do with how the teenager is really feeling. For example, many are shocked when a popular and high-achieving student commits suicide because they simply failed to see the victim's deeper turmoil.

How others see victims and how victims see themselves are often quite different.

Powerful feelings of depression may stem from, or are exacerbated by, crisis situations at home or school. Divorce or family disharmony, breaking up with a boyfriend or girlfriend, falling victim to a physical or sexual assault, or experiencing rejection or humiliation by peers can generate or compound feelings associated with suicidal depression. Such feelings can also lead to antisocial behaviors which, in turn, produce negative responses from family, peers, teachers and others. These negative reactions of others are interpreted by pre-suicidal youth as a further sign of rejection, thus reinforcing their feelings of worthlessness and isolation.

Feelings held by pre-suicidal adolescents that their problems of living are insurmountable are often reinforced by their poor social skills. As a crisis escalates, a suicidal teenager may give away personal possessions and begin to acquire pills, knives, or firearms. He or she may engage in "suicidal gestures" by experimenting with large doses of drugs, cutting one's self, writing suicide notes, or telling others about suicide intentions. For some, a period of apparent calm or silence may ensue just prior to an attempt at suicide.

These signs are similar to a number of cues that clinicians and researchers see as signaling a cry for help. The most important sign of disturbance, of course, is a history of attempts at suicide. Unfortunately, some people think that failed attempts at suicide indicate that suicide is highly unlikely. However, many suicide victims go through the motions of trying to commit suicide many times before they finally kill themselves.

Another cue provided by suicide-prone persons is a radical shift in their behavior.   Perhaps, however, because radical shifts in behavior are indicators of a variety of personal problems, the observation of such a shift in a person is seldom seen as indicative of a suicide risk.   This is why potential suicide victims often are first seen by clinicians, medical doctors, educators or other authorities for other reasons, if they are seen at all.   Among teenagers who are identified as suicide prone, many were first referred to their school counselors because of drops in their academic achievement. The high academic or athletic achiever who commits suicide is usually a big surprise to many of his or her family or peers.

Suicide is the ultimate recognition that life is without hope and that the desires for the future are unattainable.   The emotional state of a suicidal person embodies an absence of confidence in the future in terms of their desires.   It is a sad irony that suicide is usually seen by potential suicide victims as the only way to alter their future.   The teenage boy who chooses death as the means to relieve his parents of the "burden of his existence," or the young women or men who kill themselves to make the lovers who rejected them regret their actions, are examples of drastic attempts to change a particular situation.   Perhaps this is why many researchers believe that the single most powerful deterrent to suicide is to create a sense of hope and confidence that the possibilities of a better future on their terms can be realized.

Although it may seem obvious, setting goals for self and achieving those goals gives one a sense of autonomy, self-worth, identity, and a reason for being.   It is important to note that the realization of one's goals does not have to be deferred, but can be achieved immediately.   For teenagers, success may come in the form of a weekend date with a friend, an invitation to a party, performing well at band rehearsal, or any similar small-scale achievement.

The point is that a commitment to future activities and relationships, even if they are short-term in nature, preoccupies young people. It gives them positive sustaining experiences which reduce the risk of suicide. Indeed, parents and teachers are most effective when they foster in youth a realization that satisfaction can be realized by working toward and completing both immediate and long range objectives. In teenagers, such a realization promotes feelings of responsibility and caring about what happens to themselves and to others.

MISJUDGMENTS OF ADULTS

Ironically, all too often adults unintentionally disparage or ridicule the very activities which give a teenager a sense of purpose. Various activities such as sports, hobbies, or even interest in a particular form of music, which may appear frivolous to others, often are the primary things which give the teenager a sense of meaning and hope. Being effective in interactions with teenagers means encouraging them to establish their own goals and encouraging in them a feeling that they have the power to attain those goals.

Not only do many adults dismiss the immediate goals and interests of teenagers, but adults also devalue adolescents for not holding to the adults' long-term goals. What adults value may be very different from what teenagers value. It is interesting to note that parents and other adults who do not see themselves as exploitive can increase negative pressures on suicide-prone teenagers by the character of the aspirations they impose. They set goals for teenagers that are not of the teenager's choosing. Furthermore, these caring parents may link love and affection to the success their children have in reaching parental goals. In so doing, they create incredible pressure on their teenager to "succeed" in goals that are not their child's. These parents unintentionally make their love seem conditional. Not surprisingly, many of these adolescents resort to the extreme of suicide because they feel they failed or will fail their parents and therefore will no longer be loved.

Adult aspirations for youth often require an extremely long-range orientation. Such an orientation may enhance the sense of meaninglessness, isolation, and powerlessness among teenagers, especially if these youth are denied the validity of their own short-term goals. Indeed, it is the absence of highly valued short-term goals, coupled with the imposition of adult standards, that is key to understanding much of the suicidal behavior of adolescents. Perhaps this is why a recent national study found that among high-achieving teenagers (by adult standards) as many as 31% have contemplated suicide and 14% have attempted suicide.

When one denies the legitimacy of a teenager's goals, it also produces another undesirable consequence: it reduces the likelihood of effective communication. Consider, for example, the consequences of a teenager in a crisis who feels unable to turn to his or her parents for help. Sadly, all too often the very people who should be available for assistance are seen by the potential victim as judgmental, unapproachable, and not key resource persons to seek out for help. It is a virtual certainty that a teenager will not initiate a dialogue with his or her parents if there is no prior history of meaningful communication between them regarding his or her hopes and attainments. When adolescents develop a sense that they are responsible and autonomous agents with the power to choose and to achieve their choices, the prospects of engaging in self-inflicted harm decline.

COMMUNICATION IS CRITICAL

Knowing that a teenager is in crisis is one thing; knowing how to communicate with him or her is a separate skill altogether. Effective communication is usually a precondition for prevention and intervention efforts to be successful. It is especially critical for teachers and school counselors who have regular contact with a troubled youth to know how to keep the lines of communication open. Drastic action such as running away or attempting suicide often take place in a context where communication with adults who could intervene has either broken down, or is entirely absent in the first place.

DO'S AND DON'TS

In order to establish positive communication with troubled youth, there are a number of strategies adults may wish to employ. Among these are the following:

• Refrain from trivializing the teenager's problems by indicating that he or she is "overreacting." What seems like a small matter to an adult can be momentous to a young person. Failure to acknowledge the validity of a youth's feelings or problems reduces open communication.

• Avoid the tendency to respond by being judgmental or moralizing about a teenager's feelings or behavior. Reactions of anger, irritation, or attempts to make him or her feel guilty tend to convey a message of rejection.

- Do not apply "reverse psychology" on an adolescent who is threatening to run away or commit suicide. Challenging a young person to "go ahead and do it" may be the deciding factor which compels him or her to make good on a threat.

- Resist the urge to take sides against family members. Even if family members are part of the problem, reinforcing the view of them as villains may make the troubled youth feel even more alone.

- Communicate the view that the crisis or pain experienced by the youth is temporary, that help is available to solve the problem, and that you are willing to stand by him or her until the problem is resolved.

- Reinforce the notion that the troubled youth is needed and loved, and that family and peers would be diminished if he or she were to depart.

- Do not validate feelings of hopelessness or helplessness in the teenager. Rather, convey empathy but emphasize the positive things he or she can do to gain control over the problematic situation.

- Realize your own limitations and do not hesitate to seek the assistance of others.

SUICIDE IS PREVENTABLE

While the motives for attempting suicide will vary with each individual, it is important to realize that self-destructive behavior can be prevented. It is preventable if others learn to recognize the signs given off by a suicidal teenager, if help is made available to them in a timely fashion, and if adults learn how to communicate more effectively with youth in crisis. Perhaps most important of all, suicide among teenagers can be prevented if those adults in contact with troubled youth help to "empower" them to gain control over their lives.

To "empower" teenagers means several things. It means helping them to develop coping skills to solve problems and resolve conflicts with others. It means helping them to understand and deal more effectively with their own powerful emotions such as anger, grief, fear, or feelings of guilt. It also means helping them to realize the relationship between feelings and behaviors, and helping them to manage feelings in safe ways without relying on drugs or alcohol.

Empowerment means building in teenagers a sense of self-esteem and a feeling that they are valued. This implies helping them in the recognition of strengths and limitations in self without requiring "perfection" in self. Empowerment also means providing teenagers with the skills to build healthy attachments and to reach out to others. This includes learning how to avoid overcommitments, learning how to say "no," learning how to handle "put downs," as well as learning how to ask for help. Finally, empowerment means helping teenagers to make the small changes in their daily lives which will help them to cope with difficulties and still achieve their goals.

Simply stated, empowerment is the building of skills and competencies which reduce a sense of helplessness and hopelessness. When a teenager feels empowered, he or she has a shield against the overwhelming feelings of helplessness and hopelessness which can lead to suicide. Most teenagers who attempt suicide do not wish to die; they wish to end their pain. Building competencies in them is the best way to give them alternatives to self-destruction when living hurts.

9

Reducing
the Risks

Adolscents today face perils which, if not resolved, will impose a crisis on all us, young and old. This means that we are at a crossroad. One path—the path of lassitude—leads downward to our gradual decline. The other is an uphill climb requiring changes in our systems of welfare delivery, justice and education.

Our first task is to provide better services to meet the needs of both victims and victimizers. Our second is to find ways to reduce exploitation by parents and peers in the first place. The first task requires new policies, resources and practices which affect the conduct of those who work with the abused and abusers alike. The second requires the efforts of schools.

TASK ONE: HELPING VICTIMS

Some would blame indifference, others ignorance, to explain why so few in need receive help. Yet we believe that there are many caring adults who are neither indifferent toward our young, nor ignorant of their problems. True, many victims and victimizers receive little or no help; but that has less to do with the failings of individuals than with the failings of our *system* of service delivery.

Consider the character of contemporary child protective service agencies. In communities large and small, the demand for services exceeds the ability to deliver. Why?

Child Protection Agencies

Insufficient Staff. Since the 1970s, there have been dramatic increases in the number of referrals to child protective services. Yet staff and resources have not grown proportionately. By some estimates, as few as one in ten referrals is thoroughly investigated. Even under the best circumstances, no more than half the referrals are given careful attention. As a result, only life-threatening cases tend to receive proper attention. Simply stated, a system of triage exists whereby only the most serious problems are given priority. The victims are too many, the staff too few.

Insufficient Preparation. "Baptism by fire" is the main training method of most who enter the field of child and adolescent welfare. Furthermore, neither preservice nor inservice training has been sufficient to prepare most of them for the demands of their work.

Poor Working Conditions. Another problem is that most protective service workers are embedded in work settings involving legal burdens and bureaucratic quagmires. They have excessive case loads, long hours and limited resources. Further, few receive recognition for the good they do. Their jobs are so emotionally draining that few can last more than two or three years.

Few Incentives. The conditions of low pay and low status reduce the attractiveness of the child protection profession, resulting in high turn over and reduced performance. This in turn makes recruitment of qualified personnel a serious problem. Because of poor working conditions and few incentives, workers feel compelled to quit, to transfer, or worse, they "burn out" but remain on the job without being effective.

Inadequate Resources. Improving services to those in need is impossible unless there is an increase in resources. More staff, better training and improved working conditions are essential but they cost money. Yet even with a modest increase in resources, changing the administration of services is necessary.

Dysfunctional Organization. Under the current system, protective service workers are in an untenable position. They must simultaneously perform two incompatible functions: investigation and helping.

Because of their relationship to the court, protective service workers investigate and initiate charges of abuse and neglect. Their findings influence police and court decisions about children, their treatment, and whether prosecution of parents is in order. This results in parents seeing case workers as prosecutorial investigators. Often parents view them as the enemy, not as helpers. Workers are thus unjustly cast into adversarial relationships. Being seen as an adversary is undesirable if one wants to help parents to be better care givers.

Most protective services workers know that parents need help more than punishment. Their reasoning is true and simple: help in effective parenting is needed to reduce child abuse. Once the court becomes involved, it is usually too late to be of anything more than survival help. This is unfair to victims, to their parents, to the workers and to the community.

Separate Roles. There is a partial solution. The protective service profession should be divided into two distinct and separate roles: case investigation and case work or therapy.

As the name implies, case investigators should be designated by the courts to collect evidence for legal decisions if abuse is suspected. These investigators should not assume any responsibility for the treatment of children or their parents. These investigators should be highly trained. They should have no less than a masters degree in case work, and they should have experience in working with children from abusive homes.

Different case workers should minister strictly to the needs of parents and victims. They should do no investigative tasks, and they should not be seen as the ones who determine court action. These case workers best serve as advocates for meeting family and victim needs.

The advantage in separating these tasks is obvious. Under present conditions, there is far too much stigma attached to receiving help from protective services. Rather than being open to receiving help, many abusive parents become hostile. Many recoil in fear and anger if there is the slightest inquiry into their "personal business." If the role of case worker differs from that of "police investigator," then the stigma of parents seeing childcare professionals is reduced. There is less of an implication that in receiving services, one is a criminal.

Outreach. After separating case work from investigation, enough case workers should be designated to do another critical task—outreach. Outreach means that professionals do not wait for clients to seek their services or be referred to them. It means that service personnel visit homes, schools, work environments and other locations where there is likely to be a need. It also implies actively following up on "no show" and indigent clients who are least likely to seek agency assistance. An active outreach program is an essential component to effective service delivery.

Considering the limited staff, the minimal training, and the undesirable working conditions, one conclusion is apparent: protective service workers are among the least guilty of all authorities. These workers are given responsibilities, but they have neither the training, the organization, nor the resources to do what they should.

If anyone is culpable, it is those elected or bureaucratic officials who give family welfare a low priority, allowing the protective service system to languish. To paraphrase one anonymous critic, "it is a wonder more children and adolescents don't die from a double dose of abuse and neglect – abuse at home and neglect by the government."

Changing the Law

The legal rights of child and adolescent victims of abuse often seem to be a secondary consideration in the courts and law enforcement. This statement is harsh. But how else does one explain the action of a judge who excuses an incestuous father by claiming that the daughter was being "seductive." How else does one explain why so few confirmed cases of child battering or sexual abuse result in arrest or in prosecution? How else does one explain why so many abusive parents who come to the attention of the courts are allowed to plead guilty to misdemeanors rather than to more serious charges?

One view is that attorneys seldom are trained in law school to address all the needs of victims. Perhaps this is why most child abuse legislation has come about from the public pressure of non-attorneys, rather than from within the legal profession. In addition, many legal scholars claim that the legal system functions in ways which further harm abuse victims. Even law enforcement agents recognize that the legal process can traumatize victims, thus complicating their recovery and discouraging them from pressing complaints. Whatever the merits of these criticisms, we offer a simple conclusion: if the needs and rights of victims are overlooked in the legal process, justice is ill-served.

If children and teenagers need assistance from the courts, then they should receive fair treatment and "equal protection." The task is to initiate changes that will protect people who are helpless, as well as to guarantee the rights of victimizers. These goals need not be incompatible.

Protect Rights. Our system of law enforcement—a product of our political order—seems to respond first to those who cry out and not to those who are mute. Those least likely to cry out on their own behalf are abused children and adolescents. Agents of law enforcement, along with other policy makers, need to take a more active stand in protecting the rights of victims.

The time to be particularly attentive to the rights of young victims is during the pretrial period. Many victims and witnesses experience harassment and intimidation by their victimizers, by friends of victimizers, by defense attorneys, and yes, even by prosecutors.

End Delay Tactics. Protection of youthful victims is an attainable goal. One needed change is in the scheduling of hearings. Delays are common. Court dates change often and with little notice. It is standard practice for defense attorneys to seek as many delays as possible in order to discourage victims and witnesses. The more that the courts permit dilatory tactics, the more that young victims are prevented from putting their victimization behind them and getting on with their lives.

Priorities on court calendars should go to the young who are victims. Judges can do this with no changes in the law. Our legislators, however, must provide enough judges. In too many communities, the court backlog causes delays of a year or more.

Endless delays drain any victim, but even more, they sap the strength of young people. Delays reinforce feelings of powerlessness among young victims. Their parents also feel that they are caught up in a process which both controls and dehumanizes. It is little wonder that many parents will not put their children through the trauma of what they see as "court approved" intimidation.

Use Restraining Orders. Unless there is special court authorization, criminal defendants should be ordered not to have contact with victims and witnesses. Restraining orders should be enforced vigorously. High priority should be given to investigating assertions of threat or intimidation of victims and witnesses. Proof of intimidation should be included in court records.

Courts also should withhold from defendants the addresses and telephone numbers of young victims and witnesses. Defense attorneys need not have access to victims and witnesses without approval by the prosecuting attorney or court.

The legal system should have an obligation to explain to victims what their rights are during each phase of the legal process, and to make sure that these rights are not violated. Furthermore, because criminal defendants often are released immediately after arrest, young victims usually are terrified that their attackers (or proxies of the attacker) will seek them out. Victims have a right to protection.

Give Notification. Regardless of their age, victims should receive notification before their attacker's release from a penal or treatment facility. A victim who is not notified runs the risk of unwanted encounters. Such encounters can be both traumatic and dangerous, particularly for younger victims who are suffering from a profound fear. Whenever possible, victims should know about the pending release of those who have hurt them.

Seek Alternatives. Requiring victims, especially young victims, to testify repeatedly and to provide numerous depositions is traumatic. There are experiments in various courts to provide for less intrusive procedures without hindering the rights of the accused. Examples include videotaping and having neutral parties such as judges or counselors conduct the questioning. This movement deserves praise; it reflects a growing consensus that something must be done.

Consider Impact Statements. In some jurisdictions, "victim impact" statements are being considered. Such statements by a victim or the family members of a victim attempt to document the extent of physical, financial, or psychological damage caused by the actions of a victimizer. The purpose is to affect decisions regarding sentencing and parole.

At present, victim impact statements are controversial and their constitutionality is unclear. Despite this, many people feel that they do more than merely increase the severity of punishment. These statements help victims by allowing them to feel that people are listening to their story and that the courts care.

Stronger Actions. Some advocate a bolder approach. At parole hearings, they argue, victims deserve legal representation. The intent is for victims to present relevant information (or at least have the opportunity to challenge the information presented) to the parole board. Some believe that parole boards should not allow the "exclusionary rule" to apply in hearings where revocation of parole is under consideration. Others believe that release should be tied to restitution. Whatever the merits of these suggestions, there is a shared idea that victims should have input in decisions affecting parole.

Regardless of which changes in the legal system are adopted, one guiding concept should prevail: violent and exploitive behavior is unacceptable.   Our stance, furthermore, is that victims should not be afterthoughts in the legal process.

TASK II: EDUCATION

Our best hope for helping both child and adolescent victims of exploitation in not through our protective services, law enforcement or the courts.   Our best hope is through education which teaches all students the knowledge, values and skills which reduce the likelihood of their becoming abusers.

With all that is demanded of them, however, can educators teach the competencies and inclinations to reduce exploitation? The answer is yes.   Schools can reduce exploitation if they pursue at least three major goals: providing all students with peer and other support; teaching students early and consistently appropriate values and competencies; and training all teachers to understand exploitation.

Teacher Training

Little is accomplished unless educators thoroughly understand the nature of exploitation.   This is no small task. To illustrate, consider the character of most current human development texts used to prepare teachers and other school personnel.

Until recently, most of these texts falsely portrayed nearly all students as growing up in middle class families where two healthy parents were present.   Today, human development textbooks include no more than token discussions of the dynamics and consequences of child abuse.   There is almost no recognition of the unique characteristics of adolescent abuse. While the normal aspects of adolescent development are discussed, a consideration of the nature and consequences of exploitive relationships is minimal or absent.   Hence, a thorough understanding of the social development of young people is lacking in the preparation of many professional educators.   The same is true regarding the preparation of many other professionals who work with our young.

We believe that at the very least, educators need to learn about the nature and extent of child and adolescent exploitation, how and when to make referrals, and the special problems of trying to educate students at risk.   Equally important, educators need to learn the do's and don'ts of communicating with victims and their victimizers.   Ideally, teachers should learn this before they become educators.   For now, however, the best solution is to provide effective inservice training.

Teach Early and Consistently

In order to reduce exploitation, we need to communicate to all students appropriate knowledge, values and skills from very early on.   Year after year, educators should consistently reinforce these messages throughout each student's education.

Family Living Courses.   One positive step in this direction is through the recent development of family living courses.   These courses should be age appropriate and required of all students. Many schools presently offer solid family living courses, but only a small percentage of students receive this instruction. If in the long term we are to reduce abuse, then all students must learn to recognize when others exploit them. Students must learn how to cope and to find help. They must learn how to avoid exploitation and they must learn how and why not to become exploiters.

Curriculum Integration. More important than specific "family living" courses, however, is an integrated curriculum approach where the information is simply and unobtrusively a part of other basic education. The values, knowledge and skill promoting decency can be included in the teaching of reading, writing, social studies, and yes, even math. Fortunately, there are now curricula in all subject areas designed to inform young people, from early childhood through high school, that they have rights and responsibilities. Empowering youth with such knowledge and values can improve their family life skills and is the first step toward prevention.

Peer and Other Support

For millions of our young, the family is nothing more than a place; it is not a unit of individuals helping one another. Each member seems to go his or her separate way. Even family occasions such as holidays are, for many, little more than empty celebrations. Sadly, the character of communication in these families is highly constricted (e.g., "pass the butter" or "do the dishes"), and devoid of intimacy. There is little praise or recognition of accomplishments. There is little consideration of each member's needs or feelings. Little wonder that so many adolescents, feeling alienation from their families, enter into disastrous peer relationships. For them, home is not a place of warmth.

Schools can do little to alter an unhealthy home, but they can create alternative support systems. For many of the exploited, neglected, isolated and ignored, school is the only place where they can find solace. There are millions who first came from miserable homes, but later went on to decent and productive lives as a result of the support provided by their teachers and peers at school.

Peer Assistance Groups. One positive sign is that many schools are developing "peer assistance" groups to help students with problems. Such peer support can be helpful in bringing to bear timely and appropriate interventions. While peer assistance programs are not a substitute for professional counseling, they add an additional level of help to those at risk.

There are many other examples of innovative school programs through athletics, art, drama and other educational activities. Whatever the program, our point is clear: for too many students, family life is inadequate to meet their basic emotional and intellectual needs. In such cases, school is the one place where they can acquire the knowledge, support and encouragement to recognize and to avoid exploitation and self-destruction. Society can ill-afford to have a huge portion of its young people becoming impaired, drug dependent, criminal or abusive, simply because they failed to acquire the values and skills necessary for having healthy relationships.

10

Epilogue

Exploited young people are not someone else's problems. They are real persons with names and faces—persons we see everyday. It is the boy in the neighborhood, it is the girl who lives next door, and hopefully, it is not someone in your family. All of us are affected by the countless victims of exploitation.

What must one do to reduce the exploitation of adolescents? Three areas of effort come to mind: 1) providing aid to victims; 2) reducing the exploitive behaviors of offenders; and 3) lessening the likelihood of people becoming exploitive in the first place. Clearly, the third option is the least costly and most desirable. However, what forces should be dealt with if exploitive behavior is to be reduced among friendship groups and families?

Scholars are right in believing that social and economic forces are causing an increase in parental and peer exploitation. This exploitation results in abuse, suicide, running away and other problems. Of course, no one can be sure in making long-term predictions. In the final analysis, only one source can explain this increase in physical, psychological and sexual exploitation: changes in society. One would have a difficult time attributing the recent increases in abuse to changes in heredity. Indeed, no one has ever demonstrated a genetic basis for why some parents abuse their children and others do not. That leaves only one tenable explanation: the changes that are taking place in how people live with one another.

Major changes are occurring in the family with which young people must cope. For example, more and more, children are living with multiple stepparents without benefit of proper bonding. Stepfathers and other live-in surrogate fathers have a higher probability of abusing their teenage charges than do natural fathers. Stepmothers also report special problems in relating to their stepchildren. Life is not easy for any parent, and parenting can be particularly difficult for a stepparent. Under the best of circumstances, such stresses in families are not good for children; under the worst, exploitation results.

Teenagers are also becoming more and more isolated from their grandparents, uncles, aunts, and even their brothers and sisters. Each child tends to go his or her own way. In a sense, each child becomes a stranger to the other family members. Even time spent together is not necessarily meaningful. For example, approximately half the time that families are together is spent watching television. They are together but psychologically isolated. This psychological isolation makes it difficult for parents to be effective teachers.

Where jobs once took only fathers away from their children, economic necessity is now taking mothers away. Economic forces are making it increasingly difficult for parents to be at home. For many, choosing parenthood over employment is an invitation to an impoverished life style with even more stress. And in the typical one-parent household, there is little time for the parent to be with his or her teenage child.

There are also masses of young whose parents are themselves very young and without the psychological or economic resources for effective parenting. Most teenage parents are ill-prepared for the realities of parenthood or the requirements of a career. We could go on and on, but the point is made: today family life in western culture is more likely to provide a setting for ignoring the needs of youth than was true even a generation ago.

The end result is that many teenagers, while economically dependent upon their parents, are looking elsewhere for emotional gratification. They are looking to (and becoming overdependent on) peer cultures, the mass media and the analgesics of entertainment and drugs. Some social critics feel that the end result is a culture whose members are increasingly narcissistic and self-absorbed. Such immersion into self-gratification becomes one basis for the exploitation of others.

The conclusion to be drawn is obvious: the problem of exploitation is cyclical. Abuse and exploitation are often a precondition for future abuse and exploitation. In a sense, the pattern mirrors itself and the past becomes prologue.

There are high costs to individuals in the cycle of victims becoming abusers.   There are physical and mental injuries, mental disorders, drug dependencies, impaired and unproductive workers, abuse of the elderly and individuals who are simply unable to cope with the normal demands of living.

When a large proportion of the people in a society suffer in their personal lives, democracy becomes threatened.   Simply stated, democracy requires an intellectually, economically and psychologically healthy body of citizens.

With consequences for democracy in mind, we again return to the vexing questions of how we can halt the growing number of exploitive parents.   Obviously, trained professionals cannot go directly into all of our homes to teach adults how to be good parents.   This would violate all that democratic societies hold dear in regard to personal rights and family freedoms.   Furthermore, it will be too late if we wait until people are adults to try to teach them to be decent to one another. By then, the damage is done.

If teaching parents is not the answer, what then?   How do we decrease the growing number of parents who physically, sexually or psychologically exploit their children?   There are two socializing institutions which can have an effective impact on the family: religion and education.

It is not anyone's prerogative, however, to direct the teachings of other people's religions.   If churches and temples teach their members to be non-exploitive, so much the better. But it is not appropriate to impose upon a church or temple what it will teach.

On the other hand, the public schools in a democracy belong to the public. The public has the right to expect that its schools promote the competencies and literacies that sustain it. A democracy implies an acceptance of certain core skills, knowledge and values.

Among these values are those regarding what is proper for parents to do in raising their children. Before they are parents, people need to learn that when they exploit their children, the consequences are drug abuse, peer violence, impaired competencies and other forms of personal disorganization.

Personal disorganization on a large scale will result in a breakdown of law and order, disorganization of group life, and very importantly, a breakdown in social cohesion——what philosophers refer to as the social contract. Social cohesion around a compatible set of democratic values is critical for a democracy to exist. In other words, how parents treat our young is important for the kind of society we desire. The one vehicle for effecting parenting that is subject to public policy is the school.

It is beyond the capability and scope of this book to suggest in detail all of the things that the schools or we as individuals might do to reduce exploitation in the first place. Each of us, however, will be part of the problem or part of the solution. As parents, educators, laborers, therapists, grandparents or whatever, our activities differ, but our objectives for young people should be the same. We need to help all young people:

- reduce any inappropriate feelings of helplessness;

- increase their relationships with nonexploitive people;

- manage their feelings of guilt, anger and mistrust;

- learn how and in what way they or their peers can be or are being exploited;

- acquire the skills and motivation for extricating themselves from exploiters;

- develop their abilities for dealing with exploiters when it is not prudent or possible to break off such relationships; and

- find avenues of support where they can talk about what has happened to them, without fear of reprisal or stigma.

The burden of helping teenagers at risk is to be shouldered by all of us. All of us need to have non-exploitive relationships with our mates, children, parents and peers. When we do, abuse does not occur. When we do not exploit others, others in turn are less likely to be exploitive. That is how the cycle of violence and intimidation in society can be reduced; it is how we can avoid creating more victims. Drug abuse, suicide and other self-destructive acts are symptoms. Such human misery can only be reduced when our institutions are effective in teaching parents, and parents-to-be, the value of not being selfish.

Appendix A

Resources

Al-Anon/Alateen Family Group
Headquarters, Inc.
    PO Box 182
    Madison Square Station
    New York, New York
    10159-0182

Alcoholics Anonymous World
Services, Inc.
    PO Box 495
    Grand Central Station
    New York, New York
    10163

American Anorexia/Bulimia
Association, Inc.
    133 Cedar Lane
    Teaneck, NJ 07666
    (201)836-1800

American Association of Suicidology
    2459 South Ash
    Denver, CO 80222
    (303)692-0985

American Council for Drug Education
    5820 Hubbard Drive
    Rockville, MD 20852
    (301)984-5700

American Family Therapy Association
    1815 H Street NW, Ste. 1000
    Washington, DC 20006

American Humane Association
    Children's Division
    PO Box 1266
    Denver, CO 80201

American Medical Association
    535 N. Dearborn Street
    Chicago, IL 60610

Big Brothers/Big Sisters of America
    2220 Suburban Station
    Building
    Philadelphia, PA 19103

Center for Adolescent Mental Health
The George Warren Brown
School of Social Work
Washington University
St. Louis, Campus Box
1196
St. Louis, MO 63130
(313)889-5824

Child Welfare League of America,
Inc.
67 Irving Place
New York, NY 10003

Children's Defense Fund, The
122 C Street NW
Washington, DC 20001

Coalition for Children and Youth
815 First St. NW, Ste. 600
Washington, DC 20005
(202)347-9380

Cocaine Helpline
1-800-COCAINE

Do It Now Foundation
National Media Center
PO Box 5115
Phoenix, AZ 85010

Drug Abuse Council
1828 L Street NW
Washington, DC 20036

Drug Enforcement Administration
1405 Eye Street NW
Washington, DC 20537

Family Service Association of
America
44 East 23rd Street
New York, NY 10010
(212)674-6100

Hazelden Educational Materials
PO Box 176, Pleasant Valley
Road
Center City, MN 55012

Hazelden Foundation
PO Box 11
Center City, MN 55012
(612)257-4010

International Youth Council
7910 Woodmont Avenue,
Suite 1000
Washington, DC 20014

National Alliance Center for the
Prevention and Treatment of Child
Abuse and Neglect
1205 Oneida Street
Denver, CO 80220
(303)321-3963

National Alliance Concerned with
School-Aged Parents
7315 Wisc. Ave., Suite 211-W
Washington, DC 20014

National Alliance for the Prevention
and Treatment of Child Abuse and
Maltreatment
41-27 169th Street
Flushing, NY 11258

National Clearing House for Alcohol
Information
PO Box 2345
Rockville, MD 20850

National Assault Prevention Center
PO Box 02005
Columbus, OH 43202

National Association of Anorexia
Nervosa and Associated Disorders
PO Box 271
Highland Park, IL 60035
(312)831-3438

National Association for Children of
Alcoholics
31706 Coast Highway,
Suite 201
South Laguna, CA 92677

National Association of State
Alcohol and
Drug Abuse Directors
444 N. Capitol St. NW,
Suite 530
Washington, DC 20001
(202)783-6868

National Association of Student
Assistance Programs and
Professionals
6801 Whittier Avenue, Suite 325
McLean, VA 22101
(703)448-9521

National Center for Alcohol
Education
1901 North Moore Street
Arlington, VA 22209

National Center on Child Abuse and
Neglect
Children's Bureau, Office of Human
Development Services
Administration for Children,
Youth and Families
US Department of Health
and Human Services
PO Box 1182
Washington, DC 20013
(202)755-8208

National Center for Juvenile Justice/
Research Division
701 Forbes Avenue
Pittsburgh, PA 15219

National Center for Missing and
Exploited Children
1835 K St. NW, Suite 700
Washington, D.C. 20006

National Center for the Prevention
and Treatment of Child Abuse and
Neglect
1205 Oneida Street
Denver, CO 80220
(303)321-3963

National Center for Voluntary Action
1785 Mass. Ave., NW
Washington, DC 20036

National Center for the Prevention
and Control of Rape
5600 Fishers Lane
Rockville, MD 20857

National Clearinghouse for Drug
Abuse Information
    PO Box 1908
    Rockville, MD 20850

National Clearinghouse for Mental
Health Information (NCMHI)
    Public Inquiries Section,
    Rm. 11A-21
    5600 Fishers Lane
    Rockville, MD 20857
    (301)443-4515

National Coalition Against Sexual
Assault (NCASA)
    242 Ontario Road NW
    Washington, D.C. 20004
    (202)493-7165

National Coalition for Children's
Justice
    66 Witherspoon Street
    Princeton, NJ 08540

National Coalition for the Homeless
    105 E. 22nd St.
    New York, NY 10010

National Council for the Homeless
    139 Rhode Island Ave. NW
    Washington, D.C. 20005

National Commission on Resources
for Youth, Inc.
    36 West 44th Street
    New York, NY 10036
    (212)682-3339

National Committee for Prevention
of Child Abuse
    332 South Michigan, Suite
    1250
    Chicago, IL 60604

National Committee for Prevention
of Child Abuse
    111 E Wacker Drive #510
    Chicago, IL 60601National
    Congress of Parents and
    Teachers
    700 North Rush Street
    Chicago, IL 60611

National Coordinating Council of
Drug Education
    1526 - 18th Street NW
    Washington, DC 20036

National Council on Alcoholism
    2 Park Avenue
    New York, NY 10016

National Crime Prevention Council
    733 - 15th Street NW, Room 540
    Washington, DC 20005

National Dropout Prevention Network
    4305 Illinois Avenue
    Fair Oaks, CA 95628

National Education Association
    1201 16th St. NW
    Washington, D.C. 20036

National Federation of Parents for
Drug-Free Youth
   8730 Georgia Ave., Suite
   200
   Silver Spring, MD 20910
   Hotline: 1-800-554-KIDS

National Institute on Alcohol Abuse
and Alcoholism
   5600 Fishers Lane
   Rockville, MD 20857

National Institute of Drug Abuse
   11400 Rockville Pike
   Rockville, MD 20852

National Institute of Mental Health
   National Center for
   Prevention and Control of
   Rape
   Room 6-C-12, Parklawn
   Building
   5600 Fishers Lane
   Rockville, MD 20857

National Network of Runaway and
Youth Services, Inc.
   905 Sixth St., SW,
   Suite 411
   Washington, DC 20024

National Organization on Adolescent
Pregnancy and Parenting
   PO Box 2365
   Reston, VA 22090

National Organization for Victim
Assistance
   717 D Street, NW
   Washington, DC 20004
   (202)393-6682

National School Safety Center
   16830 Ventura Blvd., Suite 200
   Encino, CA 91436

National Self-Help Clearinghouse
   33 West 42nd Street
   New York, NY 10036

National Urban League
   Child Abuse Resource Center

National PTA
   Drug Abuse Prevention
   Project
   700 North Rush Street
   Chicago, IL 60611
   (312)787-0977

National Runaway Switchboard
   2210 North Halsted
   Chicago, IL 60614
   (800)621-4000
   (800)972-6004 (Illinois)

National Urban League
   Child Abuse Resource Center
   500 E 62nd Street
   New York, NY 10021
   (212)644-6678

National Victims Resource Center
    Office of Justice Assistance,
    Research & Statistics
    Washington, DC 20531
    (202)724-6134

Office of Juvenile Justice and
Delinquency Prevention
    Law Enforcement
    Assistance Administration
    633 Indiana Avenue NW,
    7th Floor
    Washington, DC 20531

Parents Anonymous
    2810 Artesia Boulevard
    Redondo Beach, CA 90278
    (213)371-3501

Parents Resource Institute for Drug
Education, Inc. (PRIDE)
    100 Edgewood Avenue,
    Suite 1002
    Atlanta, GA 30303
    1-800-241-9746

Students Against Drunk Driving
(SADD)
    PO Box 800
    Marlboro, MA 01752
    (617)481-3568

TOUGHLOVE
    PO Box 1069
    Doylestown, PA 18901
    (215)348-7090

Youth Suicide National Center
    1825 Eye Street NW, Suite 400
    Washington, DC 20006

IN CANADA:

Addiction Research Foundation
    33 Russell Street
    Toronto, Ontario, Canada
    M5S251

Al-Anon Family Groups
    c/o National Public Information
    Box 6433 Station J
    Ottawa, Ontario, K2A 3Y6
    (613) 722-1830

Canadian Child Welfare Association
    2211 Riverside Drive
    Ottawa Ontario K1H 7X5
    (613) 738-0697

National Victims Resource Centre
Ministry of the Solicitor Gneral
    340 Laurier Ave. West
    Ottawa, Ontario K1A 0P8

Appendix B

Recommended Readings

Ackerman, Robert. *Children of Alcoholics: A Guide for Educators, Therapists and Parents,* 2nd ed. New York, NY: Fireside Books/ Learning Publications, 1987.

Adelson, J., ed. *Handbook of Adolescent Psychology.* New York: Wiley, 1980.

Ageton, Suzanne S. *Sexual Assault Among Adolescents.* Lexington, MA: Lexington Books, 1983.

Alan Guttmacher Institute. *Teenage Pregnancy: The Problem That Hasn't Gone Away.* New York: Alan Guttmacher Institute, 1981.

Apter, Steven J., and Goldstein, Arnold P. *Youth Violence: Program and Prospects.* Pergamon Press, 1986.

Bateman, Py and Stringer, Gale. *Where Do I Start: A Parents' Guide For Talking to Teens About Acquaintance Rape.* Dubuque, IA: Kendall/Hunt Publishing Company, 1984.

Barrett, Tom. *Youth in Crisis: Seeking Solutions to Self-Destructive Behavior.* Longmont, CO: Sopris West, 1985.

Bell, R., and Co-Authors. *Changing Bodies, Changing Lives: A Book for Teens on Sex and Relationships.* New York: Random House, 1980.

Benedict, Helen. *Recovery: How To Survive Sexual Assault For Women, Men, Teenagers, Their Friends and Families.* Garden City, NY: Doubleday, 1985.

_____*Safe, Strong and Streetwise.* Boston: Little Brown and Co., 1987.

Beschner, George, and Friedman, Alfred S., eds. *Teen Drug Use.* Lexington Books, 1986.

Boesel, David; Robert Crain; George Dunteman; Franicis Ianni; Marla Martinovich; Oliver Moles; Harriet Spivak; Charles Stafford; and Ivor Wayne. *Violent School Study Report to the Congress. Vol. I, 1978.* National Institute of Education, Washington, D.C., U.S. Government Printing Office.

Bolton, Iris. *My Son, My Son.* Atlanta, GA: Bolton Press, 1987.

Broadhurst, Diane. *Educators, Schools and Child Abuse.* Washington, DC: National Committee For Prevention of Child Abuse, 1986.

Brookover, W., et al. *Creating Effective Schools.* Holmes Beach, FL: Learning Publications, 1983.

Burgess, Ann Wolbert. *Child Pornography and Sex Rings.* Lexington, MA: Lexington Books, 1984.

Burgess, Ann Wolbert. *Rape and Sexual Assault: A Research Handbook.* New York: Garland Publishing, 1985.

Capuzzi, David, and Golden, Larry, eds. *Preventing Adolescent Suicide.* Muncie, IN: Accelerated Development, 1988.

Cherlin, Andrew J. *The Changing American Family and Public Policy.* Washington, DC: Urban Institute Press, 1988.

Coates, T.J., et al., eds. *Promoting Adolescent Health: A Dialog on Research and Practice.* New York: Academic Press, 1982.

Coleman, John C., eds. *Working With Troubled Adolescents: A Handbook.* London: Academic Press, 1987.

Compton, N., et al. *How Schools Can Help Combat Student Pregnancy.* Washington, D.C.: National Education Association, 1987.

Crow, Gary A. and Crow, Letha I. *Crisis Intervention and Suicide Prevention: Working with Children and Adolescents.* Springfield, IL: Charles C. Thomas, 1987.

Curran, David. *Adolescent Suicide.* Hemisphere Publishing, 1987.

Daro, Deborah. *Confronting Child Abuse: Research for Effective Program Design.* New York: The Free Press, 1988.

Doyle, A.; Gold, D.; and Moskowitz, D.S., eds. *Children in Families Under Stress.* San Francisco: Jossey-Bass, 1984.

Dunne, Edward; McIntosh, John; and Dunne-Maxim, Karen, ed. *Suicide and Its Aftermath: Understanding and Counseling The Survivors.* New York: W.W. Norton & Company, 1987.

Erickson, Edsel L. and McEvoy, Alan W. "Drug Education: Peer Pressures and Resistance," *School Intervention Report,* Vol. 2, No. 8 June 1989. Holmes Beach, FL: Learning Publications, Inc.

Farber, E.D., and Kinast, C. "Violence In Families Of Adolescent Runaways." *Child Abuse and Neglect* 8(1984): 295-299.

Farberow, Norman L. *The Many Faces of Suicide: Indirect Self-Destructive Behavior.* McGraw-Hill, 1980.

Finklehor, David. *Stopping Family Violence: Research Priorities for the Coming Decade.* Newbury Park, CA: Sage, 1988.

_____*A Sourcebook on Child Sexual Abuse.* Beverly Hills, CA: Sage, 1986.

_____*Child Sexual Abuse.* New York: Free Press, 1984.

Finkelhor, David, et al. *The Dark Side of Families.* Beverly Hills, CA: Sage, 1983.

Fisher, B., et al. *Adolescent Abuse and Neglect: Intervention Strategies.* Washington, D.C.: U.S. Department of Health and Human Services, 1980.

Flanzer, Jerry P. and Kinly Sturkie. *Alcohol and Adolescent Abuse.* Holmes Beach, FL: Learning Publications, 1987.

Frude, Neil, and Gault, Hugh. *Disruptive Behavior in Schools.* New York: John Wiley and Sons, 1984.

Garbarino, James, et al. *Adolescent Development: An Ecological Perspective.* Columbus, OH: Charles E. Merrill, 1985.

Garbarino, James and Gilliam, G. *Understanding Abusive Families.* Lexington, MA: Lexington Books, 1980.

Garbarino, J., Guttman E. and Wilson-Seele, J. *The Psychologically Battered Child.* San Francisco: Jossey-Bass, 1987.

Garbarino, James, et al. *Troubled Youth, Troubled Families.* New York: Aldine Publishing, 1986.

Gersh, M.J. *The Handbook of Adolescence: A Medical Guide for Parents and Teenagers.* New York: Stein and Day, 1983.

Ginzberg, Eli; Berliner, Howard S; and Ostow, Miriam. *Young People at Risk: Is Prevention Possible?* Boulder, CO: Westview Press, 1988.

Gross, L.H. *The Parent's Guide to Teenagers.* New York: Macmillan, 1981.

Hafen, Brent Q., and Frandsen, Kathyrn. *Youth Suicide: Depression and Loneliness.* Cordillera Press, 1986.

Hahn, Andrew, and Danzberger, Jacqueline. *Dropouts in America: Enough is Known for Action.* Institute for Educational Leadership, 1987.

Hasslet, V., et al. (eds.). *Handbook of Family Violence.* New York: Plenum Press, 1988.

Hawton, Keith. *Suicide and Attempted Suicide Among Children and Adolescents.* Beverly Hills: Sage Publications, 1986.

Hermes, Patricia. *A Time to Listen: Preventing Youth Suicide.* San Diego: Hartcourt, Brace, Jovanovich, 1987.

Hersch, Patricia. "Coming of Age On City Streets." *Psychology Today;* January, 1988.

Hodgson, Harriet W. *A Parent's Survival Guide: How To Cope When Your Kid Is Using Drugs.* New York: Harper & Row, 1986.

Ianni, Francis A. *The Search for Structure: A Report on American Youth Today.* New York: The Free Press, 1989.

Jacobs, Douglas, and Brown, Herbert. *Suicide: Understanding and Responding.* International University Press, 1987.

Janus, M.D., et al. *Adolescent Runaways: Causes and Consequences.* Lexington, MA: Lexington Books, 1987.

Johnson Institute Staff. *Choices and Consequences: How To Use Intervention With Teens In Trouble With Alcohol-Drugs, A Step-By-Step Guide For Parents And Professionals.* Minneapolis: Johnson Institute, 1987.

Johnson, Kathryn M. *If You Are Raped: What Every Woman Needs To Know.* Holmes Beach, FL: Learning Publications, 1985.

Kempe, Ruth S., and Kempe, C. Henry. *The Common Secret: Sexual Abuse of Children and Adolescents.* New York: W.H. Freeman, 1984.

Kraiser, Sherryl L. *The Safe Child Book.* New York: Dell Publishing, 1985.

Lester, David. *Suicide As A Learned Behavior.* Springfield, IL: C.C. Thomas, 1987.

Levine, Maccombie J., and Koss, M. "Acquaintance Rape: Effective Avoidance Strategies" in *Psychology of Women Quarterly. Vol.* 10 No. 4 (1986), pp. 311-319.

Lerner, Richard M., and Galambos, Nancy L., eds. *Experiencing Adolescents: A Sourcebook for Parents, Teachers, and Teens.* New York: Garland Publishing, 1984.

Maris, Ronald. "The Adolescent Suicide Problem." in *Suicide and Life Threatening. Vol* 15, No. 2 (Summer, 1985).

Mayer, Adele. *Incest: A Treatment Manual for Therapy With Victims, Spouses, and Offenders.* Holmes Beach, FL: Learning Publications, Inc., 1985.

Mayer, Adele. *Sex Offenders: Perspectives and Approaches to Understanding and Management.* Holmes Beach, FL: Learning Publications, Inc., 1988.

_____ *Sexual Abuse: Causes, Consequences and Treatment of Incestuous and Pedophillic Acts.* Holmes Beach, FL: Learning Publications, Inc. 1985.

McEvoy, Alan W. "What Price Excellence," *School Intervention Report*, Vol. 1, No. 5, 1988.

McEvoy, Alan W., and Brookings, Jeff B. *If She Is Raped: A Book For Husbands, Fathers and Males Friends 2nd ed.* Holmes Beach, FL: Learning Publications, Inc. 1990.

_____"Date Rape and the Role of the Schools," in *School Intervention Report,* Vol. 1, No. 6 (March 1988). Holmes Beach: Learning Publications, Inc.

McEvoy, Alan W., and Brookings, Jeff B. "Drug Prevention Programs," in *School Intervention Report,* Vol. 1, No. 2 (October 1987). Holmes Beach, FL: Learning Publications, Inc.

_____"Pregnant and Parenting Adolescents: Implications for Schools," in *School Intervention Report,* Vol. 1, No. 4 (January 1988). Holmes Beach, FL: Learning Publications, Inc.

_____*"Runaways and the Schools," in School Intervention Report, Vol. 1, No. 8 (May/June 1988). Holmes Beach, FL: Learning Publications, Inc.*

_____*"Sexually Abused Children: A Problem for Schools," in School Intervention Report,* Vol. 1, No. 3 (November 1987). Holmes Beach, FL: Learning Publications, Inc.

_____"School Violence," in *School Intervention Report,* Vol. 1, No. 7 (April 1988). Holmes Beach, FL: Learning Publications, Inc.

_____"Suicide and Schools: What You Should Know," in *School Intervention Report,* Vol. 1, No. 1 (September 1987). Holmes Beach, FL: Learning Publications, Inc.

McEvoy, Alan W. and Erickson, Edsel L. "Abused at Home...Beseiged at School," in *School Intervention Report,* Vol. 2, No. 5 (February 1989). Holmes Beach, FL: Learning Publications, Inc.

_____*Child Abuse and Neglect: A Guidebook for Educators and Community Leaders* 3rd ed. Holmes Beach, FL: Learning Publications, 1990.

McEvoy, Marcia. "Peer Asistance Programs," *School Intervention Report*, Vol. 3, No. 3, 1990.

McPartland, James M., and Edward L. McDill, eds. *Violence in Schools: Perspectives, Programs, and Positions.* Lexington: Heath and Co., 1977.

Merchant, Darlene. *Treating Abused Adolescents.* Holmes Beach, FL: Learning Publications, 1990.

Milgram, Gail G. *What, When, and How To Talk To Children About Alcohol and Other Drugs.* Hazelden Foundation: 1986.

National Institute On Drug Abuse. *Adolescent Peer Pressure: Theory, Correlates, and Program Implications For Drug Abuse Prevention.* DHHS Publication No. (ADM) 86-1152, 1986.

National Institute On Drug Abuse. *Adolescent Peer Pressure: Theory, Correlates, and Program Implications.* Maryland: U.S. Department of Human Services, 1981.

National Institute On Drug Abuse. *Parents: What You Can Do About Drug Abuse.* Washington, D.C.: NIDA, U.S. Government Printing Office, DHHS Publication Number ADM-1267.

National School Safety Center. "Drug Traffic and Abuse in Schools." December 1987.

Newcomb, Michael D. and Bentler, Peter M. *Consequences of Adolescent Drug Use: Impacting on the Lives of Young People.* Newbury Park, CA: Sage, 1988.

Nye, F.I., and Edelbrock, C. *Introduction: Some Social Characteristics of Runaways."* Journal of Family Issues, Vol. 1, No. 2, 1980.

Parrot, Andrea. *Coping With Date Rape and Acquaintance Rape.* New York: Rosen Publishing Group, 1988.

Patterson, G.R., & Forgatch, M. *Parents and Adolescents: Living Together.* Eugene, OR: Castalia Publishing 1984.

Peck, Michael L., Norman Farberow, and Robert E. Litman. *Youth Suicide.* New York: Springer Publishing, 1985.

Pfeffer, Cynthia R. *The Suicidal Child.* New York: The Guilford Press, 1986.

Plummer, Carol A. *Preventing Sexual Abuse: Activities and Strategies for Those Working with Children and Adolescents.* Holmes Beach, FL: Learning Publications, 1984; 1985.

Postman, Neil. *The Disappearance of Childhood.* New York: Dell, 1984.

Powell, Douglas. *Teenagers: When to Worry and What to Do.* Doubleday, 1987.

Ross, Charlotte P. *"Mobilizing Schools for Suicide Prevention."* Suicide and Life-Threatening Behavior, Winter, 1980.

Russell, Diana. *The Secret Trauma: Incest in the Lives of Girls and Women.* New York: Basic Books, 1986.

Safe School Study. Washington, D.C.: National Institute of Education, 1978.

Schowalter, J.E., and Anyan, W.R. *The Family Handbook of Adolescence*. New York: Knopf, 1981.

Sebald, Hans. Adolescence: *A Social Psychological Analysis (3rd ed.)* Englewood Cliffs, NJ: Prentice Hall, 1984.

Sgori, Suzanne, ed. *Handbook of Clinical Intervention in Child Sexual Abuse*. Lexington, MA: Lexington Books, 1982.

Smith, Judie. *Suicide Prevention Curriculum*. Holmes Beach, FL: Learning Publications, 1989.

Sorensen, James L., and Bernal, Guillermo. *A Family Like Yours: Breaking The Pattern Of Drug Abuse*. San Francisco: Harper & Row, 1987.

Straus, M.A., Gelles, R.M., and Steinmetz, S.K., *Behind Closed Doors: Violence in the American Family*. Garden City, NY: Anchor Press, 1980.

Stuart, I.R., and Wells, C.F. *Pregnancy in Adolescence: Needs, Problems, and Management*. New York: Van Nostrand Reinhold, 1982.

Szasz, Thomas. *Ceremonial Chemistry: The Ritual Persecution of Drugs, Addicts, and Pushers,* rev. ed. Holmes Beach, FL: Learning Publications, 1985.

Tobias, Joyce M. *Kids and Drugs*. Annandale, VA: Panda Press, 1986.

Tobin, Pnina and Susan Farley Levinson. *Keeping Kids Safe: A Sexual Abuse Prevention Manual.* Holmes Beach, FL: Learning Publications, 1990.

Tower, Cynthia Crossman. *How Schools Can Help Combat Child Abuse and Neglect* (2nd ed.) Washington, D.C.: National Education Association, 1987.

_____*Understanding Child Abuse and Neglect.* Boston: Allyn and Bacon, 1989.

Towers, Richard C. *How Schools Can Help Combat Student Drug and Alcohol Abuse.* Washington, D.C.: National Education Association, 1987.

U.S. Department of Education, 1986. *Schools Without Drugs.*

Vorrath, Harry H., and Brendtro, Larry K. *Positive Peer Culture,* 2nd ed. New York: Aldine Publishing, 1985.

Walker, Bonnie. *Drugs and Alcohol: A Workbook.* Holmes Beach, FL: Learning Publications, 1990.

Weisberg, D. Kelly. *Children of the Night: A Study of Adolescent Prostitution.* Lexington, MA: Lexington Books, 1984.

Young, R.L.; Godfrey, W.; Matthews, B.; and Adams, G.R. *"Runaways: A Review Of Negative Consequences."* Family Relations, 32, 275-281, 1983.